How to Be an
Urban Birder

David Lindo
Foreword by Jamie Oliver
Illustrations by Steph Thorpe

WILDGuides

PRINCETON
press.princeton.edu

DEDICATION

For Vanesa Palacios x

Published by Princeton University Press,
41 William Street, Princeton, New Jersey 08540
In the United Kingdom: Princeton University Press, 6 Oxford Street,
Woodstock, Oxfordshire OX20 1TR
press.princeton.edu

First published 2018

British Library Cataloging-in-Publication Data is available

Library of Congress Control Number 2018931647
ISBN 978-0-691-17962-9

Production and design by **WILD**Guides Ltd., Old Basing, Hampshire UK.
Printed in China

10 9 8 7 6 5 4 3 2 1

CONTENTS

Kingfisher

FOREWORD

Writing a foreword for something that's not food related is a first for me, but what a pleasure and honour it is. David Lindo is what I call a bloody legend – we met almost 20 years ago now, back in the days of *The Naked Chef*, and since then his passion for birds has soared to even greater heights. This is a great guide for anyone, and I'm really looking forward to sharing his philosophy with my kids.

David has that amazing ability to make anything bird-related fascinating, and, most importantly, a whole lot of fun! Us humans have a tendency (apologies in advance for the pun!) to pigeon-hole people, attaching clichéd traits to pastimes such as bird-watching, but David couldn't be further from those stereotypes. I love David's passion, and his belief that anyone, anywhere, should be able to love and appreciate nature and the serenity that surrounds birds and their habitats.

Being a country boy myself, my childhood was full of nature, treehouse dens, long school holidays spent outdoors, and yes, you guessed it … bird-watching! For the most part, I discovered that birds aren't super-keen on us humans, so I was always amazed when making a camp in an overturned water tank – or whatever our latest hideout was – to see how many different birds started to come out if we disappeared for a quick picnic, or just sat quietly for a little while. We learnt so much, including what sounds each bird made, and witnessed their incredible variety of colours and behaviours. I recall once seeing a kingfisher up close, and thinking that the colour and shape of its body was just as cool as the rare Ferrari we'd admire parked up outside my dad's pub.

What I'm trying to say is that you don't need to be a fully-blown bird-watcher to be inspired by David, and you don't need to live in the countryside, either – it's all about taking the time to look up and around, instead of straight forward or down at our phones. When life is so fast-paced, it's not always easy to remember to appreciate what's there in front of you, but the benefits are huge. Before they were so heavily developed, our cities were home to many birds that were sadly forced to move on; but now, even in the most built-up areas, the birds are beginning to come back, becoming savvier and adapting to new ways of living. So, guys, it's about time we start appreciating them.

Wherever you live, getting out and about and enjoying your surroundings can open up a whole new world. For me, seeing the volume of edible plants growing in all kinds of unusual places around London – the gutters of houses and flats, between mossy slate roofs, and even on busy roundabouts – is always amazing, and the same adaptability is true of our beautiful birds. Here in the UK, we're blessed with lots of parks and green spaces, so don't forget to take time out to visit and make the most of them.

Enjoy this book, and make sure you look up – deep inside all of us is an Urban Birder!

Nice one, David.

Jamie Oliver

Tawny Owl

WHAT IS URBAN BIRDING?

It's Monday, early afternoon August Bank Holiday, 2002. I am at home in Notting Hill, a fabled district of west London beloved by the ladies that lunch and the Versace pram-pushing yummy mummy set, shrine to the worshippers of 'Notting Hill' the film and the general home to cool meedja luvvies. The sun is blazing and the temperature is tipping into the hotter side of hot. It had been that way for the previous week, which is unusual for England these days. During my infancy, we had proper scorching summers that lasted, well, the whole summer. The only spoiler to this afternoon's urban bliss was a small matter known as the Notting Hill Carnival that is making its presence felt literally through the very foundations of the building. The parade is outside noisily stampeding, albeit in slow motion, down my street. This sluggish, cacophonic river is dragging with it the associated litter, bad music and a crowd of jovial humans, some semi-dressed in questionable costumes. Elements within this baying, swaying mass seemed hell-bent on relieving themselves outside my front door. Yes, welcome to my August Bank Holiday world. Surely, this doesn't happen in Rio de Janeiro?

Pembridge Road, Notting Hill

7

Call me a hater and you would probably be right. Living in the middle of its route usually drives me to escape for the weekend south to the Sussex coast to look for migrant Ring Ouzels. I had left those arrangements far too late this year, hence my presence within the mayhem. #badplanning.

I slink into the back of the house as the walls begin to reverberate with the particularly intrusive bassline of some nameless dodgy dance track. I gaze despondently through the French windows into the garden; a tiny walled affair, butting tightly onto the neighbours', covered throughout with patio slabs. You would be hard pressed to find a lick of green, but a movement caught my eye.

A male Grey Wagtail was busying itself feeding on small insects around the cracks of the slabs. As I gasped in shock at the sight of an essentially riverine bird happily feeding in my sterile inner city concrete garden, my eyes settled on yet another avian visitor. Perched on the upturned edge of one of the mini football goal posts was a Wheatear!

To the uninitiated, the Northern Wheatear, to give it its full name, is a summer visitor to the UK that is normally associated

Wheatear (male)

Nature can be nurtured anywhere.

with wilder, more desolate terrain. And even though they regularly turn up on municipal grasslands and football pitches in urban areas on migration, this one was stretching even my broad expectations. It took one look at me and flew over the wall into a neighbour's yard.

Finding a species like a Wheatear in the middle of nowhere is the accepted norm, but to find one in the middle of somewhere in a place where you would least expect them? What other amazing birds await discovery right under our noses in our towns and cities?

I was born in Park Royal in West London, not a million miles away from Notting Hill, with an inbuilt fascination for natural history. Anything with a pulse and with the ability to move caught my attention. This fascination has grown within me with each passing day. I began to focus on birds by the time I was five and after being repeatedly told that wildlife is only to be found in the countryside, and with nobody willing to take me there, I had no choice but to become an urban birder. One of the main things that I learnt (but did not fully realize until much later) was that, in the main, birds don't turn up in our cities by accident. They are there because of the habitat that is available within our growing metropolises, as these provide a haven, albeit an often disturbed and temporary one, that is forever under the omnipresent dark cloud of development.

Birds are everywhere – something I came to realize very early on. This is a phrase, and the idea, that will be repeated regularly within the pages of this book. We must remember that the notion of birds living in urban areas is by no means a recent thing. They have hopped and fluttered amongst us ever since the first societies were formed, the first brick laid, the first parking meter anchored and the first X-Factor audition held. My message is very simple: we all need to appreciate that wildlife not only occurs in our cities but it is here to stay. There is fabulous wildlife all around us and we need to encourage and conserve it in the places were it exists. Whether this be nurturing invertebrates within a tiny window box on the fifth floor of a block of flats, promoting small wild areas in our gardens, creating areas specifically for wildlife in our local parks, watching over a forgotten wild corner of our local neighbourhood or starting a green roof project. If we can learn about the importance of wildlife conservation in our cities then we will understand its connection in the general web of life on this planet, enabling us to reach out and strive to protect the rest of the world's fauna and flora and, ultimately, ourselves.

If we were to jump into Dr Who's Tardis and zip back in time we would discover that the early birders were upper class Victorian collectors who strolled the countryside in their tweeds brandishing guns and birch walking sticks. In those days the term 'birding' did not exist. People indulged in bird collecting – they 'procured' birds. This either meant shooting them in order to have them mounted and displayed in their country mansions or, if you were part of the poorer underclass, collecting finches effectively for the pet trade. Egg collecting was also rife and an accepted pastime that did not fall out of public favour until the 1970s. Thankfully, the creation of the Royal Society for the Protection of Birds during the late 1800s paved the way for effective protection of our birds, eventually changing the face of birding forever.

During my lifetime birding has now become quite a fashionable pastime enjoyed by people from all walks of life up and down the country. Several contemporary celebrities have been outed and exposed by the media as bird watchers – or more usually as 'twitchers' – as the press like to call almost anyone wielding binoculars. People like Jarvis Cocker, Damon Albarn,

Goldfinch

Alex Zane and Guy Garvey from the band Elbow have all been mentioned, along with more expected suspects like comedian Bill Bailey and politician Kenneth Clarke. Notice that there are no women mentioned. Perhaps this illustrates the media's outdated perception that it is still a male-orientated pastime. Regardless, birding is no longer seen as the hobby of choice for weirdos. It has gone from exponents being called bird spotters, bird enthusiasts and bird lovers, phrases that I have little love for, to birdwatchers, twitchers and birders. The latter term being the sexiest title if you ask me.

My Icelandic birding friends have gone a stage further and call themselves Finders. I love that. But whatever you want to label yourself at the end of the day, watching birds has got to be about the enjoyment. If you just want to watch the birds coming to your feeders that's great. If you want to build up a list and learn as much as you can, well that is great too. There is no standard to reach, no target number of species to be seen, no standardized rulebook to follow, no level of knowledge to attain and examination to pass. Birding should be about sharing knowledge and enthusing others and not just about having the best bird lists or indulging in constant one-upmanship. That said, there is nothing wrong with listing, as the act of compiling all the species that you see is popularly called. I will cover that art later in this book. Regardless, it is all about improving your ability to see, hear and enjoy more birds in urban areas than you ever expected.

Birding has journeyed a long way since the first time our prehistoric ancestors gazed up to witness groups of birds flying over. Birds have graced our planet for a very long time: scientists have found evidence of their existence since the Mesozoic Era, a geological period some 252 to 66 million years ago. That was way before the creatures that were eventually to give birth to our kind crawled, flopped or perhaps even walked out of the sea. Back then the British Isles did not exist and life in general was very different. Fast-forward to the early days of human development and birds are already featuring in our lives. Not just as menu items

but also as objects of wonderment, praise and, dare I say, enjoyment. The humble universal chicken has the distinction of being the first bird to be domesticated by man. The next species to be tamed by our hand is one of the most recognized and loathed of all urban birds: the Feral or Street Pigeon, perhaps better known by its most affectionate name, the Flying Rat!

Some of you picking up this book may be new to birding. Others amongst you may watch the birds in your back garden but consider yourselves not worthy of being called a birder. You might even occasionally go out in the countryside to watch birds on designated day trips or maybe notice birds when visiting friends or relatives in rural areas. Some of you may live in a city, town or village in the UK and perhaps never really gave watching for birds within the heart of your hometown much thought before. Well, this book could be for you. To pinch an old hackneyed cliché, I would like to take you on a journey of discovery or, to be more exact, a journey of rediscovery. It is

Feral Pigeons

11

a journey that might help you to connect more with the nature that is right under your nose and above your head. In this book I will be covering all the expected steps to becoming a birder – with a particular emphasis, of course, on city dwellers.

I would like to introduce you to the notion that to notice birds you just have to look up! Birds and other wildlife are all around us even in the heart of the most concrete of jungles. Whether you live in London, Aberdeen, Port Talbot or Newcastle, if you open a window, step out of your front door, or just stop for five minutes to listen while in town doing the shopping run, you might be surprised as to what you may discover. Very recently, I was walking in the heart of Soho in central London on my way to a meeting. It was a delightfully sunny springtime afternoon and people were out in force. Soho is the media hub of the UK and there is always frenetic activity on the streets; hardly a place to be noticing birds you might think. It is also not usually a place where you find tourists wandering its labyrinth of streets or general shoppers eking out a bargain, as they all tend to inhabit Oxford Street farther to the north. The day that I chose to stroll the streets was a classic one. There were young runners busily going about their errands for the masses of media companies based in the area, with parcels under their arms or pushing hand trolleys. Runners are easily recognizable as they tend to wear an unofficial uniform that features fashionably 'distressed' jeans and worn-looking t-shirts, regardless of what company they work for. The good media folk were out of their offices early, garrulously drinking outside the trendy bars in Golden Square in the heart of Soho. People were in the tiny park at the centre of the square variously catching the last rays of the sun or playing table tennis on the public tables.

Common Buzzard

Whilst soaking up this bustling scene I was aware of a slight movement in my peripheral vision above my head. Looking up I was delighted to witness a Common Buzzard drifting south fairly low. I stopped and just stood in the middle of the street marvelling at the majestic raptor as it slowly headed over. To think that just minutes earlier it might have been soaring in the skies over the Hertfordshire countryside to the north but was now over the centre of my city on its way to who knows where. I was spellbound. Of course, no one around me took a blind bit of notice until I produced a camera to take shots of my find. Even then they were looking at me probably assuming that I was shooting location pictures for some new movie. Nobody looked up to witness my buzzard. Although currently being our most common bird of prey in the UK they are still deemed as country birds. But they quite clearly traverse our cities and are even breeding on the outskirts of the capital. This kind of moment happens far more regularly than is reported and that is because we don't look up often enough in the expectation of this kind of thing happening.

I suppose what I am saying is that when it comes to urban birding you have to expect the unexpected, regard the unexpected as expected. Get to know the usual birds very well and then start looking for the unusual amongst the usual. That way you will always be open to seeing interesting birds and your radar will always be switched on.

Many would-be birders are put off by the idea of referring to themselves as birders for fear of being singled out for being a fake or not being knowledgeable. Certainly, when I was a kid I had the impression that anyone with a pair of binoculars lashed around their neck knew what they were talking about and, as a consequence, knew far more about birds than I ever would in a thousand lifetimes. I was a little intimidated, that had to be said, but as a super-inquisitive child I also sought out those birders to pick their brains and to learn from them. I began to realize that not everyone I approached was who I thought they were. In later life I found out that some people used an armoury of expensive optics and cameras to give the impression of great knowledge. So do not be put off. Coming across as not being knowledgeable and therefore looking like an idiot is an innate fear that simply should not exist. Nobody knows everything about anything. The more mistakes you make the more you learn and nobody makes more mistakes than the real experts.

My hope is that after reading this book you will realize that it so easy to enjoy urban birds, whether you just watch them from the kitchen window or feel the need to rush out to be the next major ornithologist. The key thing to take away is that birding is relaxing, fulfilling, enlightening and most of all fun!

So get out there and don't forget to look up!

HOW TO USE THIS BOOK

This book is about urban birding – a guide to being a city birder. My hope is that it will help you to learn the basics of how to go about watching birds in urban environments. As we have already seen, urban birding has been in existence for some time but birding specifically in cities has only been recognized as a distinct activity perhaps in the last 20 years. I believe that urban birding will be a major gateway to engaging city folk in nature for generations to come. The aim of this book is to demystify the act of birding in cities and to expose it as a fun, modern and productive pastime. It is also my aim to put across the idea that you can also contribute to conservation. This book does not necessarily follow the route that most other 'how to be a birdwatcher' books take. It is a little more organic than that, roughly following the path I took from being a young boy with a passion, to being a slightly older boy with a load more passion! If you have never really considered watching birds before, and certainly not within a city, I would like to pique your interest and have you believing that you really can find birds wherever you may be.

Urban birding is cool. Birding is cool. Birds are cool and you are cool to watch them. It is a passion that lifts me on a daily basis, along with millions of other people around the world. The great thing about birding is that it is so easy to get involved. There are many 'how to start' birding guides out there, but this will be the first to introduce city dwellers to watching birds in urban areas. If you are looking for a guide to the birds that you can find in the towns and cities of Britain you will not find it here. Nor will it be closely examining the evolution and physiology of birds. Those subjects are more than adequately covered in

other books. This book should therefore be used in conjunction with those publications in order to furnish you with any specific detail you may need concerning the species that may be mentioned.

This is not a step-by-step guide and the order of progression does not have to be followed meticulously, as you can get involved at any point. Although it will be slightly more logical to start at square one and progress to being a fully plumed urban birder, you can jump on and off at any point. Of course, not everyone goes from A to B. However, my hope is that there will be nuggets of information and a few handy tips that might help you to really get into birding. I will revisit topics during the course of the book to emphasize the fact that, as with everything in life, you start with the basics and add to that knowledge. A good example is how to take notes on the birds that you are seeing. At first these notes would be very basic and eventually, as you gain more experience, they will become much more detailed – perhaps incorporating sound clips and images. Some people start off as urban garden birders and remain as such, only really wanting to be able to identify the visitors to their gardens. That is totally fine. Others, though, jump in at the deep end chasing after rarities and building lists from the get go. That is good too. Wherever you want to take your interest in birds, I would simply like to encourage you to become more aware of the amazing nature that is all around us – even in the heart of a bustling city.

House Sparrow (male)

THE URBAN LANDSCAPE

The British Isles is a crowded set of islands with, at the time of writing, a population of over 67 million. For thousands of years the inhabitants lived in small rural communities – but the dawn of the industrial revolution was a complete game changer, resulting in people flocking from the countryside to the newly growing cities in search of work and a better life. With the best prospects for employment now being in and around the expanding cities, the exodus continued to gain momentum and more and more folk resettled within the fledgling metropolises. This expansion led to land development, house and factory building, and roads, all with associated pollution. The once green fields, ample woodlands and abundant marshes were bludgeoned out of existence along with their wildlife. The central areas of many of the cities became wildlife-free zones, instead occupied by squalor, concrete and smog.

You would think that conditions in these expanding urban areas would hardly have been conducive for birds and urban birding. However, amongst this acerbic environment some birds managed to scratch out a living. House Sparrows were very much a part of inner city life, nibbling at the copious amounts of grain spilled from the nosebags of the many work horses that were used to drag carts and carriages. At the beginning of the 20th century, W. H. Hudson, an Argentine-born but by then London-based naturalist – and arguably one of the first urban birders – wrote about the abundance of the cheeky sparrows that occupied every street corner, vociferously playing a major part in city life. They were so common that despite the Sparrow Clubs formed to cull large numbers of this familiar species, which was deemed to be a pest, they were still viewed as too common to bother looking at. If W. H. Hudson was around now, he would be surely be horrified by the dramatic drop in numbers that the cheeky Cockney Sparra has suffered, not only in London but also across the rest of Britain.

Many people today have the view that there is no wildlife to be seen in towns and cities, and, to be honest, you really do have to open your mind to the possibility of what can be found among the bricks and mortar. It may take time to tune in to the natural rhythms of an urban area but, by taking a seat in the local park or relaxing in the garden, you will gradually get hooked into the wilder side of city life. Basically, as an urban birder you will have to learn to retune your ears. You will soon start to hear birds calling and perhaps see a few fly by. This is just the start, though. The real secret to noticing birds in urban areas is to try to view towns and cities as another type of habitat.

Robin

It may not be as rich in wildlife as an estuary, stretch of pristine rain forest or savannah, but is still an important resource for birds and other animals to nest, rest and feed. Eventually you will begin to see buildings as rocky outcrops filled with crevices and ledges that are fantastic perches for birds. You will start to imagine that the bramble patch in a city centre that you are looking at is actually no different from one on an uninhabited island. That is how birds see the habitat that cities provide, and once you have locked in to that mindset you will start noticing birds that you never expected to see.

Some people find the thought of watching birds in built-up areas incongruous. The notion that a Willow Warbler, which is a common summer migrant that also breeds in remote Scottish forests, could exist in a city park may seem alien to some. To get your head around this you will need to start thinking along the lines of how a bird might see a city

Urban London

environment. Ignore people. By that I mean do not be shy to brandish a pair of binoculars in front of people. You are not naked so people will not be staring at you too much. Imagine instead that you are in the middle of the countryside just looking for birds, with other people just a vague presence. Members of the public will generally be curious, often asking if you have seen anything interesting or if you are a twitcher. Birding is a very different proposition to what it was, say, 40 years ago when the pastime was viewed in the same light as train spotting or stamp collecting. Of course, I mean no disrespect to the devotees of those noble hobbies but nowadays birding has a far more contemporary image, with urban birders at the forefront of this new movement.

Today there are about 25 million homes throughout the UK. Although a proportion of these are situated in the countryside, the vast majority are in urban areas. Indeed, over 80% of the nation's population lives and works in cities – a situation that is reflected globally. The world's population is rising alarmingly, depleting ever more of the earth's precious remaining natural habitats. There are at least 4,000 towns and cities in the world with populations of over 100,000, and it is predicted that by 2050 at least 75% of humankind will be living in cities. It is strange, but as soon as we live together in tight communities we almost immediately lose connection with nature. This disconnection seems to be almost universal. I was surprised to meet people living in the city of São Paulo, Brazil, who a few years previously were rural farmers scratching out a meagre existence. Overnight they seemed to have forgotten their roots, very swiftly becoming mesmerized by televisions, smartphones and other material goods. Soon, they too were throwing litter on the ground and readily joined in with the 'live for yourself and the moment' urban culture.

But all is not lost. Firstly, we have to accept that the towns and cities we live within will continue to expand and some may eventually become megacities. We also have to accept that there will be losses in the natural world, with habitats wrecked and wildlife displaced. This is almost inevitable. However, we can still make space for nature in our cities. Simplistically speaking, it is possible for town planners to design conurbations with sustainability in mind. Plenty of green spaces could be created, with flourishing wild flowers, and watercourses where reedbeds and other riparian vegetation are encouraged to grow.

If living walls and green roofs were actively promoted, and new buildings designed with pre-positioned holes and crevices for birds, bats and insects, the world would definitely be a better place. I saw something that comes close to resembling this utopia in Milton Keynes, Buckinghamshire. Lambasted for being 'roundabout central', I guess at first glance it may appear that way. But it is an astonishingly green conurbation. Apparently, there are four trees to every person and the town is riddled with cycle paths, parks, green corridors and lakes – lots of lakes. Milton Keynes is indeed the city of lakes. The town's 89 square kilometres has large areas of housing, commercial properties and one of Europe's largest shopping centres, requiring the creation of balancing lakes to deal with the excess rainwater runoff. The combination of woodland, riverside parks and lakes provides a contiguous green corridor that dissects the town. I had to tip my hat to the town planners. You may call me a dreamer. Perhaps I am. But just imagine if we all did our little bit to help by creating wild areas in our neighbourhoods. We could make an amazing mosaic of habitats linking our urban centres with the surrounding countryside and beyond. Within Milton Keynes, it is already happening in some places – and that is part of the reason why, in certain towns and cities worldwide, some wildlife is thriving.

Some property developers are becoming increasingly aware that people who are connected to nature enjoy healthier living – both mentally and physically. For example, one well-known developer and Aylesbury Vale District Council worked closely with the RSPB to develop a 250-acre site in Kingsbrook, Aylesbury in Buckinghamshire. It was this particular company's largest development in the UK and reflected their emerging strategy of building housing with net gains for wildlife. The result of this partnership was a housing estate with over 800 Swift nestboxes, fruit trees planted in many of the gardens to form a contiguous orchard, and hedgehog highways between every garden. There is also a sustainable urban drainage system that forms pools and small lakes, as well as wildflower meadows and verges. Badger crossing points have even been factored in to the planning of the estate. Kingsbrook sounds like a great place to live!

Another great example of sustainable development is London's Olympic Park, in London's east end. The site sits on land that was originally part of a large, derelict expanse littered

Modern Housing development, Milton Keynes

with ancient and decrepit factories whose presence blotted the landscape like ugly cold sores. Interspersed amongst this decay were greasy garages and unkempt scrubland. It was a proper no man's land. I remember the area well as an 18 year-old visiting a girlfriend in nearby Stratford. Back in those days, to visit her in the council estate where she lived meant traversing this lawless expanse, running the gauntlet of dodgy feral dogs and even dodgier feral people. En route I would stop to quickly scan the terrain, primarily for birds but keeping a keen eye out for the aforementioned potential adversaries. I was once blessed with a passing Cuckoo, but the

Swift

birders that I have since contacted about this area spoke nostalgically of regular Cuckoo and Snipe sightings plus the relative abundance of scrub warblers such as Whitethroats.

Fade to black. It is 2012. London has been awarded the 2012 Olympics and the land has had a makeover in readiness. You would have thought that it would have spelt the end for the wildlife in the area. Of course, there were no doubt casualties but in the main it could be argued that a greater diversity of life has been attracted in. As inviting as the past scenario might have appeared, in the cold light of day the area was a cesspit of poison. Most of the vegetation consisted of invasive species like Hogweed that was growing on soil riddled with contaminated toxic waste. From day one, the vision for the Olympic Park was to build a complex that fused sustainable biodiversity with human needs. I visited the site in 2011 when it was still under construction and was very impressed with the level of care and thought that had gone into the landscaping and naturalizing of the park, that adjoins with the Olympic Village itself. The Olympic Park contains more than 2,000 specially selected

Olympic Park Velodrome, London

native trees, planted with both people and nature in mind. Many of the structures, including the bridges that span the adjacent River Lea, have been fitted with nesting holes for species as varied as Kingfishers, Sand Martins and bats. The Wetland Bowl, riverside woodland and reedbed in the northern part of the park were established using vegetation sourced from East Anglian fens. Even the actual village itself, constructed with its low-rise buildings and stadia to house the world's athletes, was designed with nature in mind.

The makeup of most cities and towns generally seems to follow the same simple planning blueprint that lays out the use of land and the design of the urban environment. Public amenities, transportation networks and the research, analysis, mapping and architectural design of the communities all form part of the strategic thinking. Thrown into this mix are watercourses and other bodies of water, woodlands, gardens and other often very fragmented habitats that are so crucial for wildlife. Sustainable development is slowly creeping into the game plan of today's urban planners. It's a movement that I personally welcome as our modern lifestyles increasingly use up too many natural resources, create too much pollution and, critically, destroy precious ecosystems.

So it is possible in an ever-growing urbanized world to at least put a bit back towards nature. But what of our British towns and cities as they stand now? Are there really localities for us to enjoy birds within the mass of concrete? Many of our urban birding locations are essentially relics from the past: islands of natural and, sometimes, not so natural habitats like woodlands, rivers or grassland that have somehow survived despite suffering from man's interference. Some of these places have no official protection and, although viewed as oases by resident birders, often attract the attention of developers who seem hell-bent on concreting them over.

To discover the wealth of birds that can be found in urban areas, it is very helpful to be able to recognize the various habitats in which they live.

Kingfisher

Gardens

We British love our gardens and often take great pride in making them a reflection of how we view our own little private empires and ultimately ourselves: our house is our castle, our garden our kingdom. I think that Thomas More beautifully summed up what gardens mean to us in his book Utopia: 'The soul cannot thrive in the absence of a garden.' My childhood memories of being at home are filled with the incessant sound of manual lawnmowers, barking dogs, kids playing and sparrows chirping. My garden was a sanctuary that I retired to after school, if I was upset and, most of all, when I wanted to be close to nature.

Robin

Although gardens have been in existence since the time of the Romans, the private household garden that we all know and love has been a fairly recent development. Essentially, we have been swanning around in gardens since the Victorian era. Initially, woodland birds like Blackbirds and Robins were enticed out of their gladed cover to forage in this newly created habitat. For these species and the others that followed, gardens were a halfway house between their natal

Suburban area, Norwich

woodland homes and forest clearings, albeit bordered and framed by alien concrete structures inhabited by people.

Gardens are a very important resource for wildlife and are a major contributor to urban biodiversity. They provide nest sites and feeding areas not only for our birds but a whole plethora of wildlife. You cannot have an interest in birds without being aware of the plants upon which they perch and feed, and the range of insects, mammals and other wildlife with which they interact. No one component can exist without the other, no matter how small and insignificant they may seem.

It is estimated that about 87% of households in the UK have gardens that, combined, cover more than 1,670 square miles (or 4,325 square kilometres). That's a huge area – a little over a fifth the size of Wales, and more than all our nature reserves combined. Although flat-dwelling is more of a feature of our cities than elsewhere, even in London around 61% of households have a garden. The usual scenario is that inner city areas tend to have small, rather run-down gardens, while the farther out you go the more extensive and luxuriant they become. But even in the neglected gardens of city centres life can abound, especially if nature is in control. For instance, research has shown that House Sparrow populations are more prevalent in these areas than in and around the manicured larger gardens of the more well-to-do suburbs. Generally speaking, the less aesthetically pleasing the garden the more likely it is to be attractive to wildlife. The mosaic of gardens across our cityscapes has led to the oft-quoted fact that our British gardens combined support more biodiversity than the mighty Amazon jungle!

However, the rise of the paved-over back garden to make way for patios, the concreting over of front gardens to accommodate cars, and the spread of neat gardens, heavily manicured with featureless lawns and planted with insect-repelling ornamental flora has sounded the death knell for much of our urban garden wildlife. I truly believe that many households simply do not realize that the more manicured the space, the more sterile it is for nature. People genuinely believe that wild looks messy and that you can't beat neat. I also believe that many gardeners do not understand how easy it is to bring wildlife into their gardens. I love looking at back gardens while riding the overground train system around London. This reveals, to my dismay, the proportion of gardens that feature large squares of boring mown lawns, sterile patios replete with plastic furniture and dull wooden fencing that make the gardens look utterly ugly. I have even noticed gardens with artificial turf laid down. Why? On a journey I make regularly on the Metropolitan line between Baker Street and Pinner in north London there are, however, a few wildlife-friendly gardens to be seen. Most seem not to be deliberately designed as wildlife refuges but instead happy accidents, as they tend to look unkempt with disorderly clumps of bushes and long grass. I can imagine the host of invertebrates thriving within the greenery along with resident Hedgehogs and nesting Wrens. Unfortunately, some of these gardens are liberally blighted with dumped piles of unsavoury garbage, evidence that these unkempt oases are purely accidental.

Since I have left home my mum has made a third of her garden into a patio and a now rickety wooden fence has replaced the hedge that used to harbour a Blackbird nest for years. But to give her credit, she has left most of the remainder of the garden as it was. When I

visit I usually pop upstairs for an obligatory nostalgic scan of the nearby backyards. I am pleased to say that despite the changes to both my mum's garden and the neighbours' plots there are still a few birds to be seen, although the House Sparrows have gone.

Gardens are great spawning grounds for would-be birders. They are very often the first place were people notice nature, as was the case for me. The provision of food is always a great strategy for bringing birds into your garden and nearer to you. Some of the garden birds will become acquainted to your presence, most famously Robins, and will allow quite close approach. I will look at the ways of attracting birds into your garden a little later on.

Blackbird chicks

Public parks

Our modern neighbourhood parks are another Victorian invention. They were initially created as areas of open space set aside for recreation. If you look further back in history then you would find that many of today's larger parks were originally tracts of land used by the aristocracy to hunt boar and deer. The bigger the hunting grounds, the greater the wealth and status of the owner. London's Hyde Park and the adjoining Kensington Gardens is a great example of parkland that began life in the 1500s as a deer park, after Henry VIII

Wren

had it confiscated from a monastery. It was eventually opened to the public in 1637 by Charles I and is today seen as the quintessential British park. Some of those hunting grounds eventually evolved into landscaped gardens, perhaps the most famous being those sculptured by landscape architects such as Capability Brown. But as the surrounding metropolitan populations expanded, these former hunting grounds became domains for the general public to roam.

The rise of the Industrial Revolution gave parks a whole new meaning, as they became areas set aside in our urban centres where the local populace could embrace nature. The earliest purpose-built urban park was created in Toxteth, Liverpool in 1843; then a quiet, well-heeled locality, a far cry from what it is today. The park was laid out according to the vision of gardener and architect Joseph Paxton, who went on to design The Crystal Palace for the Great Exhibition in London in 1851. His blueprint of ornamental grounds designed around a lake formed the basic plan for parks to come and he is often cited as a principal influence in the design of New York's Central Park. Landscape design was all the rage in Victorian days, with parks being created as an oasis of green from the clogged and polluted city streets. Some of our more famous British parks were borne from this era, including Liverpool's Sefton Park, Birmingham's Handsworth Park and Sheffield's Endcliffe Park.

Our public parks were not so revered by the 1970s and 1980s, when many local authorities relegated their maintenance to the bottom of their list of priorities. As a result, quite a few became festooned with litter and dumped vehicles, and turned into no-go, crime-ridden areas. Thankfully, that situation was largely reversed in the 1990s when money was put into improving local parks to create safer environments that people would want to visit. Also, the committed involvement of active local communities helped to facilitate the survival of many parks. This has been so successful that there are now estimated to be 2·5 billion visits to parks in the UK every year.

Princes Park, Toxteth

Most parks share the same features, although those in poorer inner city areas can, by virtue of their location, sometimes be small and quite run-down. There will be trees that, in the worst-case scenarios, are planted as avenues or, more helpfully for the urban birder, as a wood. Even in the most sterile of parks with a few randomly planted, lonely looking trees amid fields of concrete you may still discover the occasional roving tit flock, the odd crow or two or, if you are really lucky, a migrating warbler that has stopped briefly to glean food from the foliage. It is always worth exploring these areas of green wherever you find yourself near one. Even the most basic of parks can still have something to offer the urban birder. I remember being in a minute, nondescript inner city park in Birmingham yet enjoying great views of Blue Tits, Greenfinches, a pair of Mistle Thrushes and a gorgeous singing Goldfinch. All this in a park surrounded by buildings and a busy road. These tiny green areas are usually sited in highly urbanized areas, frequently on a single vacant building plot or on erstwhile derelict land, and are often referred to as pocket parks. They are also sometimes created as part of a bigger building project or new housing estate. Pocket parks are fantastic conduits for getting local communities together and are often actually administered by the local people. Despite their diminutive size they can still be worth popping into, even if it is just to watch Robins and Blackbirds.

Of course, you would stand a much better chance of discovering birds if the park you visited contained wooded areas. Although small, these 'woodlets', for want of a better word, can sometimes harbour a relatively rich ecosystem, especially if the undergrowth is allowed to prosper and the wood itself is managed. Apart from being home to many insects it may well serve as good feeding and nesting places for Blackbirds, Song Thrushes, Robins and tits.

Many public parks also feature some kind of watercourse, be it a lake, pond or river. Such lakes and ponds are often ornamental and sometimes concrete edged, precluding the existence of waterside vegetation. One classic concrete-edged urban pond is the aptly named

Mistle Thrush

29

Hyde Park and Kensington Gardens, London

Round Pond in Kensington Gardens. It is usually swamped with tourists from all the corners of the globe who come with their kids to feed the swans and feral geese. Wild duck were not slow to populate this medium-sized pond and there is always a large swarm of gulls during the winter begging for scraps from the visitors.

It is the gull action at Round Pond that attracts urban birders because sometimes amongst the more familiar Black-headed and Herring Gulls there is a hidden gem. One of the local birders discovered inner London's first Ring-billed Gull, a rare transatlantic vagrant to Britain. More regular was a beautiful Mediterranean Gull bearing a German ring on its leg. With its completely white wings, it differed subtly from the similarly plumaged Black-headed Gulls. This bird spent several winters in London and was eagerly awaited each passing year.

There is absolutely no vegetation on the pond or around its shores, yet one autumn a juvenile Ruff was discovered walking around the edge busily feeding and mingling with the pigeons and Starlings. This wader probably fledged from a remote eastern European marsh and ended up in London having flown off course during its southward migration. It had no fear of humans, sometimes walking within inches of its admiring audience, perhaps indicating that we were the first people it had ever seen. I have watched many Ruffs before but this was the closest I had ever been to one: right in the heart of a capital city.

Quite a few ponds and lakes are stocked with ornamental waterfowl. Not an urban birder's idea of heaven you would be forgiven for thinking. But even in this circumstance

Ring-billed Gull (right) with Black-headed Gulls   Mute Swan

Teal

you can still learn a lot from the captive birds residing there. I used to visit St James' Park in central London quite frequently as a kid to study the exotic ducks and geese that begged for bread from the passing public. My rationale was that one day, when I was able to visit my roots in the West Indies, I might see the Bahama Teal that I had been studying here for real, and if I did I would recognize it instantly. Watching these tame birds also allowed me to study the truly wild duck species that would turn up to join the feeding bonanza, particularly in the winter. I would count the wild Tufted Ducks and Pochards amongst my Bahama Teals, South African Shelducks and Bar-headed Geese. In more recent years, planners have been designing and creating lakes and ponds that have natural edges fringed with reeds, willows and other waterside vegetation. This is great habitat for invertebrates such as dragonflies and also provides good nesting spots for Mute Swans, Moorhens and Coots, as well as smaller riparian birds such as Reed Warblers. Even in heavily visited parks with larger lakes used in part for boating there still can be little corners for wildlife.

An occasional glance at a watercourse in your local park, even segments that have been used as a dumping ground, can pay off, as you may see a Grey Wagtail picking its way around the rusty, semi-aquatic scooters or shopping trolleys looking for insects, or a Moorhen swimming around the flotsam, deploying their classic head jerking movements. As a kid, Monks Park in Wembley was my local stomping ground and the murky, concrete-bedded River Brent ran through it. Over the years, despite the garbage in the river, I still saw a fair number of birds along its course, including Kingfisher, a wading Common Sandpiper and Teal. I'm happy to report that within the last ten years Brent Council has restored the park and re-routed the river, giving it a more natural meander. It looks a far better place for wildlife now, and is a far more pleasant place to walk through.

Grass is a prerequisite for any parkland, although all too often it is mown to within an inch of its life. This often results in boring expanses of lawn marked out as sports pitches or used by the local residents as sites for sunbathing or picnics during the summer, and for ball games and dog walking throughout the year. But even these seemingly ornithologically sterile fields can occasionally draw wildlife. During the winter, gull flocks might form first thing in the morning to loaf before being disturbed by the first of the dog walkers and joggers. Starlings and Canada Geese may also gather to probe for insects and graze respectively, while Pied Wagtails and very occasionally migrant Wheatears might be found. Over the years on the expanse of grass at Wormwood Scrubs I have even recorded such oddities as shorebirds like Curlew, Whimbrel, Common Sandpiper and Oystercatcher, and I have seen a Kingfisher flying low across the football pitches on at least two occasions. These kinds of visitations by birds must occur on sports fields across the nation more frequently than is imagined.

Some public parks have designated wildlife areas ranging from patches of grassland that have been allowed to seed, through wildlife gardens to full-blown nature reserves. These are the areas to make a beeline for, as they may well be the most attractive for birding. Try walking through one as part of your daily journey to work or school. You will get to know the regular birds – but one day you may find yourself getting in late. That will be the day when you discover something really interesting!

Wheatear (male)

Rivers and canals

There cannot be a town or city in the entire UK that has not got a river or canal running through parts of it. With 2,200 miles of rivers and canals in Britain, there is a lot of habitat to explore. These watercourses are valuable sites for urban bird life, although the character of the watery habitats they support can be highly variable. Some urban rivers are tidal, whilst others have been dammed. The banks of some have retained their natural attractiveness, although many have been moulded by the hand of man – scoured of their riparian borders and their very life force altered by the drainage of chemicals and waste products. That said, many rivers have been cleaned up and their ecosystems monitored by the various river authorities, trusts and local volunteers. Sheffield is a shining example of how its riverine ecology was rescued from the brink after being seriously polluted by the heavy industry of the past. Now a walk along the city's rivers can be rewarded by engaging views of Grey Wagtails picking at insects from the aquatic vegetation and Kingfishers perched patiently on the overhangs. And if you're lucky you can even happen across Dippers.

Although the success stories are many, there are problems. Britain's rivers are prone to clogging by foreign plants such as Water Fern or Floating Pennywort that are spread by people disposing of them irresponsibly. Our rivers are also plagued with alien invaders like the all-pervasive American Signal Crayfish that damages banks with its burrowing and carries a disease that threatens our native White-clawed Crayfish. These problem species, along with other unwanted alien plants, are currently estimated to cost the Canal and River Trust in excess of £700,000 per year to manage. Non-native invasive species generally are a massive threat to our native wildlife, and are estimated to be costing the UK economy up to £1·7 billion a year.

River Orwell, Ipswich, Suffolk showing urban redevelopment in the Wet Dock

Tidal rivers are perhaps one of the most exciting areas to watch for birds, especially when the tide is out and the muddy foreshore exposed. There is a good chance that you might discover a wader like a Common Sandpiper teetering along while probing for invertebrates or, more likely, a Grey Heron standing like a sentinel at the water's edge. I enjoyed studying a section of the Thames near Tower Bridge in Wapping, east London back in the days when I had an office job. I saw several of the common species of gull on a daily basis, and on more than one occasion witnessed parties of migrating Sandwich Terns – a bird that you normally come across by the coast. The outfall from power stations and other industry that runs into rivers can also make for potentially exciting birding, especially as you become more experienced and particularly during migration periods. Sometimes good numbers of gulls and terns assemble, attracted to the fishes that shoal in the warmer waters.

But regularly visiting a patch along almost any part of a river that you live near could be rewarding. Aside from Mute Swans, Tufted Ducks and Mallards, which in themselves are fascinating creatures to watch I must add, you may catch sight of unexpected birds like Reed Buntings or, if the weather gets really cold, a Water Rail. I use the word 'unexpected' with my tongue firmly in cheek because you may find that those unexpected birds are, in reality, more regular than you originally imagined. Even if the river looks unappealing at first glance don't dismiss it and give it a few goes. I always hark back to my childhood spent birding and looking for sticklebacks along my local stretch of the River Brent in Monks Park, Wembley. Once heavily polluted, it is now a completely different proposition with a much cleaner water quality. OK, there may still be the occasional crisp packet that floats downstream but there are also plenty more Moorhens to look at now.

Try not to be prejudiced by the location of the bit of river that you are looking at. Even the centre of town has something to offer. I remember being pleasantly surprised at the superb water quality in some of the inner city streams that I came across in Glasgow, Manchester and Middlesbrough. The unfrozen burn (a stream to non-Scotsmen) that I visited in Glasgow has even been known to attract the extremely elusive winter-visiting Jack Snipe. Perhaps the most

Mallards

famous inner city riverine birding experience in Britain has got to be the breeding Kittiwakes on the Tyne Bridge in the middle of Newcastle. These seafaring gulls are normally found breeding on cliffs and on the ledges of buildings by the coast. They then spend the rest of the year out at sea as far away from land as you can possibly get. They are proper seagulls. The Newcastle Kittiwakes are the world's most inland colony; right in the middle of a city.

Canals are another very familiar feature of the urban landscape in Britain. We were the first nation in the world to deploy a national canal network. Again, stemming back to the Industrial Revolution, these man-made watercourses were built for the vital purpose of transporting raw materials and finished products. At that time the road system was in its infancy and the legions of horse-drawn carts were the Eddie Stobarts of their day. After the Second World War competition from the emerging road haulage industry put paid to the usage of all but the largest canal systems. But even they eventually buckled under the pressure of competition from road haulage and many fell into disrepair. Canals began to be viewed as areas for recreation during the 1960s, and by the 1970s enthusiasts nationwide were restoring their stretches of canal for narrowboats. This gradual restoration was also a fillip for wildlife. Far from being sterile troughs, many now resemble rivers, albeit non-meandering ones, some occasionally with decent riparian habitat lining their banks.

The urban world looks very different when you stroll along the towpath of a canal. Sometimes you feel that you are out in the country when you come across beauty spots with plenty of overhanging willows. In really urban areas, though, you are much more likely to come across stretches were the concrete banks are the main feature and the industrial backdrop still present, if a little dilapidated. But even amidst this apparently barren scenery there are birds to be seen. Moorhens, Coots, Mallards and Canada Geese are a given, but I have also seen Kingfishers, Lapwings, Grey Wagtails and even a Little Ringed Plover while cruising on a narrowboat on the very urban Manchester Ship Canal.

There is certainly some very good urban birding to be had anywhere along Britain's canals. I live very close to the Grand Union Canal, a 137-mile waterway linking London

Kittiwakes (adults and chicks), Newcastle, Tyneside

A stretch of canal in Croydon

with Birmingham. Whenever I nip to the local supermarket, which is situated right on the canal at Ladbroke Grove, I usually spend a few minutes scanning for birds. Although I have yet to register my first Waxwings in the car park, I do enjoy sifting through the gulls that congregate by the water's edge particularly during the winter. It is really nice to watch shoppers engage with the birds by throwing them pieces of bread. Unbeknown to the shoppers, they are actually doing me a massive favour by drawing in the gulls from miles around, enabling me to scan through them close at hand, ever on the look out for a scarcer species among the throng.

Reservoirs, gravel pits and lakes

Some of my most memorable urban birding moments have occurred when I've been birding around man-made bodies of water. Despite their artificiality, they seem to become 'naturalized' and populated by wildlife very quickly. Even disused gravel pits quickly fill with water and can immediately become special places for wildlife in general. Some of these areas of water are often a tremendous magnet for birds – and not just the ones that like floating on it or stalking around it. The associated habitats provide great nesting areas for smaller birds and the water itself is, of course, important for drinking and bathing. Gravel pits are singularly the best places to see birds in an urban area, attracting a wide range of species. And, as a result, they are brilliant places to learn about birds and urban birding.

Every town and city has at least one body of water that could be of interest to the urban birder. Reservoirs are often the biggest in size but they can be a bit of a mixed bag. Some are utterly amazing, filled with tons of duck and gulls during the winter, and being a major attraction for wading birds during migration. On the other hand, you may find other seemingly identical reservoirs that, on closer inspection, appear to be devoid of life. Some reservoirs are merely concrete bowls with no natural edging and provide little by way of food for any passing duck. Others are too small to attract flocks of wildfowl, and yet others have too many human activities like yachting and windsurfing going on for it to be a suitable environment for wildlife. A scouting trip to your nearest reservoir will therefore be needed to ascertain its attractiveness for birds. However, before doing this, check to make sure that access is allowed to the general public, as many reservoirs are the property of regional water boards. Although you might find that your local site has restricted access to the public, all is not lost as many water boards have a friendly attitude towards birders and may grant you a permit if you apply. The lack of general visitors is often a good thing, as this usually means that these important bird habitats get little disturbance and are wonderfully peaceful places to visit.

Black-headed Gulls

Canada Geese

Woodberry Reservoir, London

The first reservoirs were built in the UK in the early part of the 19th century, around London at Ruislip, Elstree and Hendon. My first proper local patch was at one of those original reservoirs: Brent Reservoir in Hendon, north London. When it was originally constructed it was out in the sticks, outside London itself, but by the time I found the place in the mid 1970s it was completely surrounded by busy roads, housing and factories. The Brent was, and still is, a true urban birding oasis. I used to watch breeding Skylarks and Reed Buntings going about their business during the summer, plus the site also boasted breeding Tree Sparrows – a species that is so rare now in urban London. In winter, I would marvel at the many wintering waterfowl that would show up, and be especially on the lookout for Smew, a stunning and highly localized winter-visiting duck from Scandinavia. The Brent at one point was the place to go to see this scarce duck and coachloads of birders used to converge on my patch to see them. I guess that you can tell that I am about to say: "well, things are different now." And you would be right. The Smew have all but gone and Skylarks no longer breed –but the Brent, for the time being, still has other great birds to see, despite the continual pressure imposed upon it by developers.

Some reservoirs have been designated as nature reserves, or are at least partially managed with nature in mind. Often they may have anchored rafts put out to attract nesting terns, and have the occasional hide sited near the water's edge to allow for closer observation of the waterfowl. It is quite incredible to see how nature adapts to some entirely man-made vistas, using the unnatural materials that dot this landscape to their advantage. Coots often use bits of plastic to make their nests, Sand Martins breed in artificial nest burrows, and Kingfishers regularly perch on exposed pipes or wooden stakes when hunting. Even the concrete shores are worth examining for the possibility of a migrant wader, like a Common Sandpiper picking its way along the waterline.

Coots nesting on floating rubbish

As I mentioned earlier, some deep reservoirs, even though they may have unattractive stark, concreted edges are very important for holding good numbers of wintering waterfowl. One example is the reservoir complex in the Colne Valley in west London. These reservoirs, along with some of the nearby gravel pits that have been allowed to fill with water, are rich in vertebrates and fishes – a major draw for many species. The deep water is also a safe place for these birds to congregate for their nightly roosts, when they are often joined by flocks of gulls. Although

Black-headed Gulls

such gatherings provide an excellent opportunity to get to grips with the identification of these birds, at the very least, it's just great to watch and admire the waves of birds arriving raucously on a cold evening to settle on the water. If you decide to adopt a reservoir as your local patch you may discover that there's already a bird group actively managing and watching the site – so introduce yourself and get involved in its conservation.

Gravel pits and quarries are fascinating places to explore. They sometimes appear a very alien landscape populated by monstrous, driverless JCBs, eerily quiet and seemingly abandoned mid-dig. All this set against artificial cliffs and pits. The scenario that I have been describing is a rather illicit one, as working pits are dangerous places to visit and are usually strictly out of bounds. Please do not be tempted to trespass onto them, and only view

Little Ringed Plover

Kingfisher

London suburbs

them through the outer perimeter fence. However, once they become disused and filled with water they sometimes make the transition to nature reserve. When wandering around one of these reserves, it is often very hard to imagine what they looked like in their previous existence. Little Ringed Plovers, the slightly smaller and highly migratory version of the more familiar and mainly coastal Ringed Plover, were one of the first birds to take advantage of this newly created habitat in the late 1930s.

Lakes and ponds are also prevalent in the urban environment, but despite appearances surprisingly few are actually natural. For the sake of simplicity I will group ponds as smaller versions of lakes, even though I've seen huge ponds and tiny lakes in my urban travels. Ponds tend to be in peoples' back gardens and, as such, serve a very different purpose for the would-be nature watcher. I will examine their role more closely in the Urban garden birding section. Although ponds also occur in parks and woods, perhaps most familiar is the archetypal village pond complete with quacking ducks. In urban areas, small ponds in parks seem to be the domain of frogs and are crammed with a variety of invertebrates, beloved by small pond-dipping kids. Unfortunately, such ponds also seem to be much loved by imbecilic fly-tippers.

Proper lakes tend to be more public by virtue of their size, although some, of course, are on private land. The advantage that lakes have over reservoirs is that they have normally been designed for ornamental purposes, and are therefore often more ascetically pleasing to the eye than concrete-edged reservoirs. They are also much loved by the angling fraternity. Urban lakes often have natural edges and sometimes an island or two that act as a sanctuary for nesting ducks and geese, inaccessible to land-borne predators such as foxes. Sometimes, these islands are wooded, which is manna from heaven for urban-nesting Cormorants and Grey Herons.

It is certainly worth checking the lake situated in the park right in the centre of your town or city. Despite the bustling surrounds, there will – you guessed it – be birds to be found.

Great Crested Grebes displaying

St James' Park, within sight of Buckingham Palace in central London also sports a large lake. Although it is stocked with a lot of pinioned (clipped) wildfowl, there are always wild waterfowl to discover. It is one of the few places within central London where you can watch displaying Great Crested Grebes doing their penguin dance thing, while supping a cup of takeaway coffee. It is just incredible to be able to watch one of the most beautiful bird displays to be seen in the UK with the hubbub of city life going on all around. That is the wonder of urban birding.

Cormorants nesting at Walthamstow Reservoir, London

Woodlands and trees

It is hard to believe nowadays that most of Britain was once covered in a carpet of trees. The vast majority of this woodland was cut down predominately to make way for agriculture. The demise of Britain's woods and forests, and our lack of respect for the trees that are native to these lands make for sorry reading. The fact is that Britain is one of the least wooded places in Europe. In 2017, according to the Woodland Trust, only around 10% of the UK's land area was woodland, compared to an average of 36% across continental Europe. Although we are creating thousands of hectares of new woodland, urban woods are still being chopped down at an alarming rate to make way for development. Urban woodland is generally defined as all the wooded areas within the confines of a town or city, ranging from full-on woodland through shrub-covered areas down to individual street trees. All of these habitats can be productive for birds, although to varying degrees. It is always worth peering up into a street tree in the hope of seeing something interesting perched or foraging in the canopy – that is if the tree is anything other than a London Plane (I'll explain more later). I've often noticed migrant Willow Warblers in street trees while walking to work, and there is always a Blue Tit or two busily feeding overhead amongst the foliage.

The woodlands that most of us are familiar with usually exist on the edges of conurbations, such as Epping Forest in east London, whilst inner city woods are often disguised as cemeteries or harboured within private gardens. At this point I need to differentiate between shrubby areas and shrub cover in gardens, which I will look at in more detail a little later. Shrubs provide great cover and nesting sites for many birds, and if they are berry-bearing can attract wandering winter thrushes and, potentially, Waxwings too. Woodland edges and parkland sometimes contain shrubby spots that can be well worth

investigating. Warblers are the first things to look for from spring to autumn, and at all times Robins, Wrens and Dunnocks are the avian fare to be expected.

It is well known that trees and woodlands are vital for our health and wellbeing. Nothing beats a summer walk through a gladed woodland filled with exquisite birdsong and buzzing insects. The crunch of twigs underfoot is so evocative, as is the chance sighting of a fleeing deer or a Sparrowhawk dashing through in full hunting mode, chasing some unseen quarry. In urban areas trees provide a range of critical functions. They create shade that helps to mitigate the urban heat island effect, while their leaves and roots intercept rainfall and contribute to reducing the risk of flooding. Trees also help to improve the air quality and the London Plane is perhaps our best-known urban air cleanser. Local councils love them and have promoted them as the roadside tree of choice due to their tolerance of atmospheric pollution. Despite its name, the London Plane is not a native tree; in fact it is a hybrid and has a lot of Spanish chlorophyll flowing through its capillaries. However, unfortunately it is not particularly attractive to birds since is supports little by way of insect life. The other downside of this tree is that it sheds short, stiff hairs that can be an irritant if inhaled and cause conditions such as asthma. Also, the discarded large leaves are the bane of the lives of city councils' street cleaners, as they are tough and can take up to a year to decompose. It now appears that Silver Birch has been identified as the new anti pollutant tree – a native species that is much more agreeable to attracting wildlife.

Our relationship with woodlands has changed quite significantly in recent times and a lot of the romance associated with them has been swept away, especially amongst the younger generation. This change in attitude may have been fuelled by the concept of stranger danger; a phenomenon that is a blight on today's society, causing our children to miss out on exploring and discovering woodland nature. As a child I spent hours foraging

London Plane

Kensal Green Cemetery, London

in woods near my home – making camps, looking for bugs and, of course, checking for birds. It saddens me when I, along with others, have to fight against the regular threats of the ritualized stripping of undergrowth in the scant woodlands that still remain. The reasoning is that without it potential rapists and child molesters will have nowhere to lay in wait. Although these dangers do exist, just how prevalent are they really? Is it more likely that a pair of Blackcaps would nest there if the cover were left?

Woods and forests are wonderful places to visit during the spring, especially when the dawn chorus kicks off in mid-April. The birdsong can be quite deafening at this time of year, and is one of the quintessential sounds of the British Isles. Be aware, though, that woodlands are often decidedly quieter in winter, with many of the birds moving away and into the sanctity of gardens.

Cemeteries

I used to get funny looks when I confessed to a love of birding in cemeteries, and to this day any visit to a new city will entail a visit to the nearest necropolis. I have discovered some really great burial grounds all over the country, most of which are not often visited by birders. Some, like Great Yarmouth Cemetery on the Norfolk coast, are a must for local and visiting birders because they are great places for discovering interesting migrants on their last/first landfall before they continue their journeys. There must be many more coastal cemeteries that with regular coverage could produce fantastic birds – as proved at Margate Cemetery recently when a local patch birder discovered Britain's tenth-ever Dusky Thrush that had flown in all the way from Siberia.

Tawny Owl   Green Woodpecker

The best cemeteries for birding tend to be the older ones that contain stands of ancient trees and areas of unkempt graves with good scrub cover. By their very nature, cemeteries are peaceful places that, although often situated in the heart of urbanity, are absolute sanctuaries for wildlife. The human visitors that attend these places are not rowdy but instead are quietly paying their respects: creating a tranquil atmosphere that is a great recipe for some good birding. Cemeteries should be viewed as fragments of woodland, complete with its associated wildlife. My local cemetery, Kensal Green Cemetery in west London, is a good case in point. Sandwiched by busy roads, a canal and housing, it was built in the 19th century as one of the imaginatively named Magnificent Seven Cemeteries in order to alleviate the overcrowding in the existing parish burial grounds. Within its grounds I have discovered breeding Coal Tits, Tawny Owls, Stock Doves and Nuthatches that exist nowhere else in the immediate vicinity. It has a healthy population of Great Spotted and Green Woodpeckers plus a variety of other common woodland species. I had a similar experience in Southern Cemetery in Manchester recently – a big cemetery with lots of mature trees. This is the final resting place for such luminaries as music impresario Tony Wilson, L. S. Lowry and Sir Matt Busby. After paying my respects I was soon watching Jays and Great Spotted Woodpeckers in the trees. My best sighting was discovering a Coal Tit that was nesting in a hole beneath a headstone near L. S. Lowry's grave.

Eating your lunchtime sandwich while sitting quietly on a bench in your local cemetery, or taking a morning stroll around the area will undoubtedly be rewarding. Many cemeteries will have 'Friends of' societies that organize events to help with the upkeep of the nature areas as well as the graves.

Heaths and grasslands

The official definition of a heath is open, low-growing woody vegetation established on poor-quality acidic soil. This is a relatively recent habitat type, having first evolved during the Bronze Age some 3,000 years ago as the result of forest clearance. Heathland is considered a rare habitat in Europe and although fairly extensive in Britain is rarely found in urban areas.

Grasslands, however, certainly are a feature of our town or cities. Frequently, up to a third of an urban area may be grassland, ranging from amenity grassland (lawns and recreation grounds) and agricultural pasture to 'natural' grassland habitats (including acidic grassland and chalk downland) and what might be termed 'rough' grassland. Some of these areas have gained legal protection or are designated as common land, often in combination with other habitats including heathland and scrub.

I have already touched on the avian possibilities to be discovered dwelling on your local sports fields and lawns, with gulls, Starlings and winter thrushes being the main players. However, these areas are not the first choice for most birds, and the range of species you see will be far poorer than if you visited an area of common land. Grasslands are mainly the domain of seed-eating and insectivorous birds and are worth examining for finches, buntings and, where there are patches of scrub or even isolated brambles, warblers like the Whitethroat. The value to wildlife of these locations is greatly enhanced when the grassland is not mown to death, but instead allowed to grow tall and rough and run to seed, or when wildflower meadows are encouraged. For me, there is nothing more enchanting than a beautiful wildflower meadow. Not only are they great for inspiring kids, but it's definitely hard to resist the temptation to skip gaily through them, holding hands with the person nearest you. But, as with heathland, tall or rough grasslands are often viewed as untidy and ultimately useless spaces by the general non-nature-minded populace.

Housing development at Canford Heath, Dorset

It's always worth checking out patches of heathland or scrub for the beautiful little Stonechat, which, for me, is synonymous with this type of habitat.

Nature reserves

When you think of a nature reserve, the image usually conjured up in one's mind is that of a managed wilderness, perhaps with a fence around it, in the middle of nowhere. They are essentially islands of nature within the greater countryside to which people travel from miles around to observe the species that seem to have chosen these oases as their sole hang-out. Nature reserves are the archetypal places for finding birds, and many people still believe that they are the only places to see birds – so the idea of urban nature reserves certainly doesn't always rub. However, as a nation we are blessed with quite a few urban nature reserves. Some are small patches of land crafted into a variety of different habitats that provide a great opportunity for getting the local populace into nature. Many are good places to visit, as they are relatively quiet – and are often surprisingly fruitful for birds. I remember visiting Gunnersbury Triangle, a tiny triangular patch of woodland in Chiswick, west London that is totally encircled by trading estates that butt right up to the boundary fence of the reserve. Despite its small size, standing within the reserve I felt as though I was in the middle of a delightful broadleaved woodland. Long-tailed Tits flocked with Great, Blue and Coal Tits and, best of all, I watched two female Sparrowhawks scrapping just feet away on the woodland floor, right in front of my eyes. It was an unforgettable experience.

Some urban nature reserves are quite large and well equipped for mass visitations, with hides and wardens to help you with your birding queries. The Wildfowl and Wetlands Trust's reserves, including the London Wetland Centre and the Washington Wetland Centre in Tyne and Wear, are great examples. I had an amazing experience at the Washington Centre watching the spectacle of several hundred Curlews coming in to roost, the highest urban concentration of this declining species that I have ever seen. To cap it all, a Barn Owl drifted past the hide I was sitting in, within touching distance, before pouncing on an unfortunate unseen rodent right next to me.

For some of our urban nature reserves the future is not a rosy one. Many are flimsily protected and frequently subject to the attentions of developers looking to make a quick buck, or allowed to become neglected due to budget cuts by the councils supposedly presiding over their upkeep. Sadly, this is an all too common occurrence. Wormwood Scrubs, which is also a local nature reserve, has been under constant threat during the many years that I have birded there. Before I first visited, there was a battle with the Channel Tunnel developers that the local Scrubs Wood Group ultimately lost. The defeat resulted in the woodland on the site being destroyed to make way for rail tracks and sidings. Now the danger threatening 'my' site is far greater, and from not one but three mighty adversaries: the London Mayor's Office, Transport for London and the HS2 initiative.

Long-tailed Tit

Gunnersbury Triangle Nature Reserve, Chiswick, London

Wildflower meadow in an urban area, Bolton, Lancashire

Herring Gull

Coastlines

If you are lucky enough to live in a town or city by the coast, then you have the possibility of regular sightings of gulls and waders, and perhaps see the occasional tern flock. Granted, these birds are by no means exclusive to the coast, especially gulls, which have successfully ingratiated themselves into our inland city lives. However, there is something reassuring about hearing the yelping of Herring Gulls and the repetitive "*kleep*" of passing Oystercatchers; surely sounds that could only be associated with the seaside. One of the advantages of being by the coast is that it is the first or last landfall for migrating birds, particularly if you live on the south or east coasts. Perhaps the most ornithologically exciting seaside town I ever had the pleasure of birding in was Hartlepool in County Durham. Although Hartlepool Headland is largely urban, the local patch there is effectively the whole area. During the migration seasons the streets, trees and even the houses themselves should be checked for tired migrants.

You could also indulge in watching the sea for passing birds. Depending on the season, you are likely to see various species of gull, terns such as Common and Sandwich, plus waders including Redshank, Oystercatcher and Curlew. Looking farther out to sea from a promenade or rocky point you could possibly search for Gannets as they plunge-dive after fish or, more usually, flapping nonchalantly across the waves as you admire them from the esplanade. However, sea-watching is a discipline whose practitioners are normally hardened (and weathered) birders who will think nothing of spending hours sat looking out to sea. To a normal mortal it could be a cold, soul-destroying and sleep-inducing experience, but these guys seem to have an uncanny knack of being able to put a name to even the smallest specks on the horizon.

Oystercatchers

Peregrine

OTHER URBAN HABITATS

Urban centres

The very heart of the city is perhaps the last place you would expect to find birds – or any wildlife for that matter. It is here more than anywhere else that many urbanites think the only wildlife present is dodgy humans after dark. City centres are usually where the tallest buildings are situated, and also where some of the oldest ones remain. Here, the buildings and streets are usually more closely packed together than the rest of the town or city. But even amongst this dense concrete sprawl there are birds to be looked for.

If you view the buildings as cliffs, and their cornices, sills and overhangs as ledges, then you will start seeing birds. The most spectacular urban cliff dweller is the Peregrine. In recent decades, they have really thrived in this environment, with a plentiful supply of Feral Pigeons, another urban cliff dweller, to sustain them. It has been found that although pigeons are their staple meat and two veg, Peregrines also prey on a far wider range of bird species – from Corncrakes, a very rare land-loving and migratory relative of the Coot, to Goldcrests and everything in between.

City of London

53

Peregrines love tall, prominent structures like cathedrals, chimneys and roof corners, from where they can coolly survey their kingdom. It seems as though almost every town and city centre up and down the country has its own Peregrines, and these birds provide a brilliant way of getting people engaged in nature. They inspire awe and certainly connect communities together. Ordinary people unite and are proud to follow the nesting progress of their very own local birds on the legion of webcams that have now been set up. It is incredible to think that during the Second World War there were only around 60 pairs left in the whole of the UK, as they were ruthlessly hunted by man. During the 1950s and 1960s, Peregrines suffered further declines due to the effects of pesticide poisoning, but with the banning of DDT their population slowly began to recover. Now they have discovered our urban centres as places of ample breeding sites, food and protection from persecution. At the time of writing, there are at least 1,400 pairs nationwide, with London alone boasting over 20 breeding pairs. The world's fastest animal is now a confirmed city dweller. Who was it that said there is no wildlife in our towns and cities?

Up with the Peregrines on the ledges and roof surfaces of our inner cities are the gulls. Although Lesser Black-backed and Herring Gulls are decreasing nationally at an alarming rate, they are often the default gulls of our inner cities – always to be seen sailing over if you take the time to look up. In some cities, such as Bristol, Gloucester and Cardiff, they are found breeding in large numbers on the flat roofs of supermarkets and office blocks. Lesser Black-backed Gull, when adult, is easily distinguishable from the similar-sized Herring Gull. Its wings are slate-grey with black tips and it has yellow legs, whereas the Herring Gull sports the typical 'seagull' grey wings, which have more contrastingly black tips, and has pink legs. Once you get to know this species pair you may begin to notice that the Lesser Black-back has marginally narrower wings than its congener. There is a reason: Lesser Black-backed Gulls are migratory. After breeding in our British cities, they leave the Herring Gulls behind and travel down to southern Portugal and northern Africa to spend the winter. Well, that was once the case but more of them are now staying put, hanging out in our urban areas year-round. Why travel all that way when you can get plenty of food within the city limits?

Grey Wagtails dispaying

If you come across Grey Wagtails on your travels around the centre of your town or city, do not be surprised. In their natural habitat, you would expect to see this delightfully attractive bird picking at insect life on the banks of wild, raging rivers miles from any city. Yet they have taken to urban living with aplomb, substituting the fast-flowing rivers with slower-paced canals. When I worked in Soho I used to watch a male that regularly came to an adjacent rooftop puddle to hunt for insects. He really stood out against the grey slate, which always made me think that the name Grey Wagtail is a bit of a misnomer. They really should be called 'yellow' wagtail due to their largely yellow plumage relieved by the blue-grey upperparts and, in the case of the male, a black bib. But then, there is already a Yellow Wagtail that itself would be better called the 'yellow-green' wagtail. Whilst on the subject of wagtail names, the Pied Wagtail moniker works well as a description of Britain's most familiar wagtail, However, its European counterpart is called the White Wagtail, but is hardly white; it ought to be called 'grey' wagtail. I sense that there is a bit of circularity happening here!

Rooftops

I'm a great advocate for getting onto rooftops, not least for enjoying elevated views of the city or town that you are scanning. The higher the roof the more serene the feeling you get, especially if the ascent is made pre-dawn. Watching the sun rise over a rousing city can be a surprisingly beautiful and uplifting experience. There is also the real possibility of seeing birds drifting past while you are taking in the scenery.

It almost doesn't matter where the rooftop you choose to watch birds is, and you could even watch from atop the building in which you live or work. It is not necessary to be on a recognized migration flight path, and neither is a lack of height a major problem. In fact, low-rise buildings are probably better, as a lot of birds travel at this height – so long as you have a good panoramic view that is not restricted by too many unsightly brick walls. Being up high can be great, but the higher you go the fewer birds you are likely to see – unless you scan really carefully high above your head as well as down towards street level. After years

Birding on Tower 42, London

Fieldfare

Common Buzzards

of watching for migrating raptors from the roof of London's Tower 42, I have noticed that there is actually an optimum height for rooftop birding. The roof of Tower 42 is some 600 feet above the city streets, and the majority of birds that I've seen have been flying past me between street level and the 600ft mark. I see birds much less frequently above that height, unless, that is, I lie on my back staring into the sky for long periods. On rare occasions I have suddenly picked up a lone Common Buzzard or Sparrowhawk drifting over so high that it was almost invisible to the naked eye.

The best time to get onto the nearest city rooftop is during the migration season. During the spring it's best to try and get aloft between late April and early June. However, as most of our smaller migrant birds travel by night, you are better off looking out for raptors, especially in balmy conditions with fluffy clouds and a slight south-easterly breeze. The optimum period to watch is between 10am and 3pm as by this time the ground will have heated up sufficiently to send currents of warm air skywards – creating thermals, at the apex of which, cumulus clouds are formed. Migrating broad-winged birds, particularly raptors, but also Herons and Cormorants, can use these thermals to spiral upwards as it requires very little effort on their part, and they can then glide from one to another thermal with great ease.

Urban areas are particularly good places for thermal production thanks to the so-called 'heat island effect', being up to seven degrees warmer than the surrounding countryside. The main cause of this effect is that our towns and cities are constructed using a variety of materials, some of which very effectively store short-wave radiation from the sun. This heat is stored within the concrete and building surfaces, which act as a huge reservoir of heat energy. Incredibly, concrete can hold up to 2,000 times as much heat as the equivalent volume of air. Added to this is the small amount of heat from wasted energy usage, principally from cars and industry. I get very excited on still, warm sunny afternoons because you can almost sense that a bird of prey might fly over your head at any time. A good indicator that conditions could be right for finding raptors on the move is the presence of soaring gulls. Notice them and you are well on your way to spotting a raptor drifting over.

Cormorant

Scan the skies carefully and you may see a bunch (or to be more technical, a 'kettle') of circling Common Buzzards that might otherwise have passed over unnoticed. They are a delight to watch as they circle majestically on the thermals. Birds of prey are by no means easy to identify specifically, as they are a set of birds that require hours of observation before you can really start to tell your Common Buzzard from the much rarer Honey-buzzard. That said, you could simply just enjoy the sight of a raptor shifting its quarters over a cityscape without worrying about its identity. Essentially, that is the beauty of birding. It can be pretty mind-boggling when you start to wonder where these birds have come from, and, perhaps more intriguingly, where will they be ending up? In many instances the raptors that we notice traversing our urban areas may not be British at all, but birds heading to their breeding grounds in remote forests in Scandinavia in the spring, or to some unknown African destination during the autumn.

Rooftop birding during the autumn is a slightly different affair. The 'return migration' season starts in mid-August and runs into November. The early part of the season is still high summer for most folk, but for a birder autumn is already in full swing. Midday vigils are still the order of the day to catch sight of raptors riding the thermals, heading south, but at this time of year it is north-easterly winds that the avid skywatcher is wishing for. These are the winds that might bring the Scandinavian raptors sweeping back across to the eastern side of Britain. By late September the tactics should change to watching the skies for the first two to three hours after dawn in the hope of catching the flow of smaller birds like finches and pipits; most of the raptors having left our shores by then. It is also around this time that the first of our winter visitors, such as Redwings and Fieldfares, are winging their way into the UK, crossing the paths of the last of the summer migrants to leave.

A good substitute for standing on a rooftop is to gaze out of a high-rise window. I have spent many hours over the years watching for birds through a variety of office windows whilst pretending to bosses that I was seeking inspiration. I have also spent ages either standing on the urban balconies of friends or staring through their windows in the pursuit of interesting birds. Indoors is also a good place to be when a northerly wind whips in or if the heavens decide to open up. One thing to remember is that even in the height of summer it may be a tad cooler when you are out in the elements on the roof. So a pair of trousers and a coat would not go amiss.

A word of warning: if you think that you'll be watching floods of birds flying over your head from your lofty perch, you may be slightly disappointed. If your rooftop is in somewhere like Aberdeen or Dundee, then you might expect to see skeins of migrating geese passing over, with the occasional flock of Whooper Swans to add to the variety. However, in most other places in the UK, particularly in the midlands and the southeast, you may have to be satisfied with the occasional gull swooping around. Either way, you will be straining your eyes for any kind of movement on the horizon or low over distant rooftops. Sometimes on Tower 42 it's possible to go for hours without seeing anything other than gulls and a few Cormorants, and the birding can be an almost soul-destroying experience. But, like in football, it only takes a second to score. Suddenly you pick up a distant dot heading your way and you meticulously trace its slow progress until it comes close enough for you to attempt to identify it. Also, as with football, it's important not to take your eye of the bird, because if you do you may lose it forever – but even so, raptors flying behind a building still sometimes manage to disappear into a black hole! Once you get a bit more proficient at identifying some of the birds that you see from your high-rise vantage point, it is always a good idea to feed your discoveries into surveys set up to monitor the movement of birds. One such survey is BirdTrack run by the British Trust for Ornithology (BTO), which is an online and smartphone app for birders to log their day-to-day sightings. The information gathered from this survey is fed into the Euro Bird Portal to help provide a Europe-wide picture.

Red Kite

Sewage farms

Once the staple domain of many an urban birder, the smelly sewage farms of my youth have now become an extreme rarity. The two sewage farms that I used to visit in London were Perry Oaks and Beddington, but these have changed beyond recognition. The former site used to border Heathrow Airport and is now under a busy runway, whilst the latter, although still smelly, is less of a treatment works and more of a working gravel extraction, landfill and sludge-spreading site. Unfortunately, the future for

Tree Sparrow

Beddington Farmlands, as it is now known, looks grim. At the time of writing, there are plans for an almighty incinerator to be built on the site. It will wreck the habitat and certainly speed up the dramatic decline of the nationally scarce Tree Sparrow. The site used to boast one of the biggest breeding colonies in the UK of this mainly rural sparrow, with over 300 fledglings ringed in 2008. To put this in more graphic terms, in 2007 there were 1,000 birds present; by 2013 only 15 remained.

Back in the day, we used to run our raw sewage directly into the nearest river, but during the latter half of the 19th century sewage farms were established to improve water sanitation. In recent times, most of these farms have either been closed down or modernized

Sewage farm, Whitlingham, Norfolk

and reduced in size. Birds are generally attracted to these sites once the sludge tanks have been flooded, and gulls may sometimes pick at the edible floating debris. Once the tanks are empty Starlings and Pied Wagtails flock to take advantage of the insect life attracted to the muddy pools, squabbling under the shadows of swooping Swifts, Swallows and House Martins, all also keen to make the most of the insect feast. Indeed, I recently peered through a fence at a sewage works in Warrington and witnessed at least 300 Swifts swirling over the treatment tanks.

In common with gravel pits, sewage farms are not usually the sort of place for urban birders to be found wandering around uninvited. They are strictly out of bounds and usually only viewable through the perimeter fence. But, if you can find a good vantage point, you may be in for great treats like large flocks of Starlings, roosting Pied Wagtails and passage waders. But I must say that for beginner birders there are many easier places to watch birds.

Marshes

Throughout the lowland areas of Britain there are sometimes areas of land that have become waterlogged, resulting in the development of marshes. Today, this is yet another extremely rare habitat that within urban environs is unfortunately becoming even rarer. The continual threat from urbanization and agriculture has never been far way. Marshy conditions can be found around the edges of lakes and large ponds, and in the floodplains of rivers where water meadows, scrub and wet woodland – consisting of birches, Alder and various willow species – may develop. Ordinarily, you can expect to discover breeding Sedge Warblers, Reed Buntings and other small woodland birds in such areas. Marshy ground can also occur on industrial and disused land, and is always worth a look. I have surprised myself at such sites by flushing unexpected Snipe and discovering breeding Lapwing.

Little Egret – a recent colonist from Europe and now often seen in marshes across southern Britain.

Salt marshes are another variation on the theme and may be found in or close to towns or cities situated near the mouth of an estuary. This is a rich ecosystem, running between higher land and open salt or brackish water, that is regularly flooded by the tides. Worldwide, it is a severely threatened habitat, with development being the key enemy. Just as an example, the Bay Area of San Francisco has the last remaining fragment of half-decent salt marsh in California. Although still good for birds, the area must once have been an amazing place, as more than 90% of the original marsh has been lost under concrete. Salt marshes are irresistible to wildfowl and waders, and large numbers may sometimes congregate.

Brownfield land and building sites

You would probably be hard-pressed to call brownfield land or building sites habitats, let alone expect such places to be good for birds. Ordinarily, they are out of bounds so as to not encourage trespassers – so peering through fences will be the usual order of the day.

Brownfield sites are normally areas of land cleared for the construction of commercial property, and are usually sited within trading estates. With the recent recession, work was temporarily halted on some of these sites, allowing them to become colonized by plants and leading to the formation of small pools of water. I have visited many brownfield sites, but for me the most memorable ones were in the centre of York and in a trading estate in Leicester. Despite it being surrounded by ugly warehouses, I found the site in Leicester to be particularly lovely. Once you blanked out the depressing industrial surroundings, you found yourself looking at a wilderness. It was a fenced-in mini-marsh with waterside thistles replacing the expected reeds; an undulating landscape largely covered in lush grasses gave the area an almost natural feel. Several Pied Wagtails chased after insects, a Snipe and a couple of Jack Snipe lurked in the patches of thicker vegetation, and, best of all, during the summer a pair of Little Ringed Plovers was also in residence – a species that is synonymous with wasteland.

Building site at Lysaght Village, Newport City, Gwent

Conservationists are now urging developers to conduct environmental impact assessments before building on brownfield sites, as some, like the one I visited in Leicester, have become 'naturalized' and at least locally important for wildlife. These areas can indeed provide 'wild space' for local communities in urban areas.

Building sites are even harder to sell as possible birding venues, but bear with me when I suggest that when walking past one during the summer it is often worth having a quick look. Most building sites are very ugly places with no wildlife-attracting redeeming features. However, sometimes

Black Redstart (male)

the most unsightly of urban habitats can be absolutely magical for birding – and manna from heaven for a singing male Black Redstart. It is surprising how this little bird's scratchy song can lift above the sound of the pneumatic drills and shouty workmen in their hard hats. The Black Redstart is a master of unobtrusively eking out a living in building sites and other derelict areas. The nucleus of our current breeding population resides in London, Birmingham and the Black Country, with other tiny enclaves scattered among a few other urban centres. I used to work in east London and remember one year discovering a singing Black Red, as they are affectionately named by birders, as I walked past a building site on the way to my lunchtime patch by the Thames. I monitored it during the course of the summer, knowing full well that by the following summer its territory would be lost – under a block of luxury apartments.

There is a certain transient feel to these areas that, on the one hand is pretty sad, but on the other hand shows how readily and quickly nature takes advantage of the opportunities that do arise.

Little Ringed Plover

Landfill sites

Historically, the most commonly used method of waste disposal was to dump it wholesale into a landfill site. City dumps were recognized as places that attracted wildlife, and produced bad smells. During the winter months especially, landfill sites were a major attraction for gatherings of gulls. These birds sometimes numbered in the thousands and flew in from miles around to enjoy the edible delights strewn amongst the general rubbish. However, since the 1980s, Britain has toed the European legislative line and most landfills are now operated as full containment facilities. Associated with this, many sites have introduced a no-food policy and householders are now asked to deposit edible refuse in composting bins. No doubt this will have an effect on the numbers of scavenging gulls and crows, but it seems highly unlikely that these species are entirely reliant upon this food source and will instead disperse around the general area.

As with birding around active gravel pits and building sites, wandering around landfill sites without special permission is an absolute no-no. It goes without saying that literally slipping on a banana skin on a landfill site could end in tears. Quite a few sites can be viewed safely from the perimeter fence in order to sift through the gulls – which brings me neatly onto the specific type of birding that people tend to get up to on landfills. It is all about the gulls. The birders who watch them tend to be totally obsessed, spending hours trying to work out the various species present by examining closely the often-minute plumage details of individuals within the multitude of milling birds. Gulls belong to the bird family Laridae and are often referred to as Larids by passionate 'gullers' whom themselves are also known as larophiles. In short, unless you want to major in the identification of gulls or just enjoy watching large groups of them, then you may prefer to visit other urban areas to watch birds.

Gulls at a landfill site near Cambridge

Shopping centre car parks

This is a relative newcomer on the urban birding scene, and doing your weekly shop can now take on a whole new meaning. The best time to engage in ornithology while humping heavy shopping bags into the boot of the car is during the height of winter. At this time of year, flocks of Waxwings can potentially pour onto berry-bearing trees and bushes, such as rowans and cotoneasters, that have been so thoughtfully planted by the supermarket developers. These fantastic birds often allow a close approach, providing great point-and-shoot photo opportunities. Throughout the rest of the year you might find House Sparrows vying with Starlings and Feral Pigeons for the scraps that we discard. Black-headed, Common and the larger Herring and Lesser Black-backed Gulls will also be visiting on the lookout for easy pickings. For me, though, the classic car park bird, be it shopping mall or petrol station forecourt, is the Pied Wagtail. Look for them feeding on the tarmac as well as pecking around on the mown grassy verges.

Waxwings

Airports

An odd choice you may think, but some of Britain's airports can be very interesting places to observe birds. They are usually situated on the edge of conurbations and often surrounded by marshland or bordered by the sea. I am not just referring to the Heathrows and Gatwicks of this world, but the tiny ones like Orkney's Kirkwall or medium-sized places like Inverness Airport, which can yield a birdy surprise. Crucially, the land surrounding our major airports is usually impenetrable wetlands and open ground that is totally out of bounds. Since 9/11, security is now ultra-high, and rightly

Carrion Crow

so, with the airport authorities taking a very dim view of any would-be trespasser. With this stringent banning of casual human visitation comes the inadvertent creation of unofficial nature reserves. Heathrow is a prime example, with its environs including reservoirs, balancing pools, woodland and grassland. In my days as a juvenile birder, long before the advent of modern-day terrorism, I would regularly breach the fencing around the now-defunct Perry Oaks Sewage Farm that lay within the curtilage of the airport and right under the flight path of thundering 747s. It was a legendary place that had a roll call of rare birds that could compete with almost any 'big' site in the UK. Sometimes, however, my illegal urban birding expedition at that smelly patch would be cut short when I had my binocular straps felt by the long arm of the law. The fear evoked by the sound of sirens emanating from the local constabulary's panda car was not only just felt by burglars caught red-handed!

Heathrow Airport

Nowadays, there are a few areas very close to Heathrow in the Colne Valley that are classed as nature reserves. But when I'm at that airport I often spend the time while sitting in a plane waiting for it to take off watching for birds that frequent the strips of grassland between the runways. Starlings and Carrion Crows often come up on my radar but I have also glimpsed Skylark and Lapwings. Grasslands are an obligatory component of an airport's environs and are always worth a scan. If you live near a small local airport why not pop over to take a look. Perhaps you might find a wandering winter flock of Golden Plovers, a passage migrant Wheatear or Pied Wagtails hanging out during the summer.

It must be stressed that not all airports are good news for the environment and wildlife. Plans to create a new airport in the Thames Estuary would have had an apocalyptic effect on the region's wildlife, and damaged a site that is internationally important for thousands of waders. Although this outrageous proposal has now stalled, the danger is not yet over from other proposed developments such as the plans for expansion at Lydd Airport in Kent. Building new airports inevitably involves the destruction of the natural habitats that were once there – which, of course, has obvious negative repercussions for their associated wildlife.

The sky

Finally, this is perhaps the one habitat that a lot of birders tend to forget about. A lot of people simply do not look up, either in their daily lives or when out birding – it is the one place that most people simply do not even notice. However, a surprising array of species can be seen winging their way across our urban spaces if we only took the time to look up. And it does not have to be a sunny day either. Visible migration is often apparent in the sky wherever you may be. Even at night in winter, if you look up you may become aware of Redwings passing overhead. One night, I even saw a Coot fly over at rooftop level in west London, illuminated by the streetlights. I have always found it fascinating to watch from an upstairs window as members of the public walk down the street. It is very rare that anyone looks up and notices me; most people seemingly being content to go through their daily life looking straight ahead or down at their feet.

Birds have wings and are inclined to fly, so you really need to look up to notice them. Try to spend more time lying on your back in the park staring into the sky. If you do this, you may remember how beautiful the clouds were from your childhood, and the different shapes into which they morph. While watching aircraft and vapour trails criss-crossing the sky you might notice a bird drifting across your field of vision. By lying on your back the sky becomes a spacious arena, a wide vista that is crossed by many birds flying in all directions. Feral Pigeons will flap through either singly or in groups, as might Wood Pigeons. You may see gulls gracefully wafting over, sharing their domain during the summer months with roaming parties of screaming Swifts. In the past, I have spent time flat on my back within grassy clearings in Epping Forest and noticed migrating Sparrowhawks and Common Buzzards, birds that I would never had been aware of ordinarily. But it is not always a case of being on your back simply to notice birds, as too much of it can be sleep-inducing – which in itself may not be a bad thing!

Try to look up more in your daily life. I could fill an entire book with stories of the interesting birds that I have seen while looking up, but one of the most poignant moments was when I was walking to Notting Hill tube station one balmy afternoon in May. The streets were thronged with west London luvvies all intent on looking their trendiest best, checking their shoes and making sure that their outfits looked cool in the reflections in the shop windows. Meanwhile, I was walking, looking up, filled with expectation. It wasn't long before I spotted a Common Buzzard drifting over. One of the local crows also noticed the buzzard and didn't waste time in mobbing it furiously. A spectacular dogfight ensued: a primeval struggle that had been acted out over aeons was now happening right over the modern streets of Notting Hill. I looked around to see if anyone else was watching this amazing natural event. But no, the luvvies were busy loving themselves and checking their shoes, and the tourists were garrulously asking for directions to the bookshop on Portobello Road that was featured in the film Notting Hill. I was alone as usual, lost in nature in the middle of the city.

Black-headed Gulls flying into roost

WHAT IS AN URBAN BIRD?

If you stopped someone in the street to ask them to name an urban bird, they would almost certainly come up with pigeon. After that, a few of those people may struggle and offer up a sparrow into the mix and then perhaps draw a blank. For an urban birder it is quite simple: an urban bird is one that shows up within the confines of a city or town, however briefly. It could be a species that is particularly prominent in urban areas, like our friendly street pigeon, or one that is mainly found in habitats well away from urban areas like the Gannet – a maritime bird that nests on inaccessible rocky coastal cliffs during the summer and spends the rest of the year on the wing over the open ocean. Granted, this is an unlikely bird to turn up inland, yet every year one or two are spotted over cities like London, blown in by fierce weather conditions farther out to sea. Of course, Gannets are not proper urban birds, but they are clearly a slim possibility while out urban birding on an autumnal day. So long as you believe in the maxim that anything can turn up anywhere at anytime, then your urban birding will know no bounds.

Black Redstart

In the UK there are perhaps three truly urban bird species. The first is the Ring-necked Parakeet, an introduced species and a relative newcomer to the urban scene. Then there is the humble House Sparrow. The other is that denizen of disused buildings, and favoured Peregrine snack, the universal Feral Pigeon. The Feral Pigeon is the only species that relies almost wholly upon man for food and lodgings. Pigeons are what ornithologists term as synanthropic – ecologically associated with humans. How many Feral Pigeons have you seen in the heart of the countryside, miles from the nearest discarded crust of bread? If you have seen one, it would likely be by a rugged Scottish or Irish coastline – in which case you were probably observing the Feral Pigeon's natal ancestor, the Rock Dove, now a rarity in the UK.

I mentioned earlier that Feral Pigeons are sometimes referred to disparagingly as Flying Rats by city folk. The term 'Flying Rat' first appeared in a New York Times article in 1966, but was actually popularized by Woody Allen in his 1980 film Stardust Memories, in which he referred to these pigeons as rats with wings. Along with their non-flying mammalian namesake, they have got to be the most hated feathered creature in the land, surely? Pigeons poop whenever the desire takes them, with little respect for the unfortunate souls who might be standing underneath at the time. They certainly foul the pavements below their nest sites: classically underneath railway bridges or in deserted buildings in cities.

Feral Pigeon

I used to hate pigeons but in recent years have mellowed and grown to like them a lot. Nowadays, I actually feel sorry whenever I see a squished pigeon on the road. Even so, I do fall short of using the word love when expressing my feelings about them. The persistent monotone cooing from a pigeon secreted somewhere outside a bedroom window on a Sunday morning after the night before can be highly annoying. However, as birds, they are pretty glorious. They are magnificent flyers, not bad looking close up and pretty intelligent to boot. Plus, they provide ever-present takeaway food for city Peregrines. The fact that they are keeping our Peregrines well fed means that they get my vote. There are just too many of them on our streets, right? Well, the British Trust for Ornithology (BTO) tells a different story. Feral Pigeons have actually taken a dive in numbers in England, with a 20% decline between 1995 and 2010. Nationwide, there are estimated to be just 540,000 pairs, which means that they are easily outnumbered by the five million or so pairs of Wood Pigeon – their rotund former country and now relatively newly urbanized brethren.

There have been many studies and surveys conducted of urban birds, some of which have come back with surprising results. Pigeons are one such fascinating subject matter. For example, research has shown that they are able to recognize the faces of the people that feed them, even if those faces are in a crowd of others. In London, some have learnt to ride the tube system, seemingly purposefully disembarking a few stops later to continue nonchalantly pecking at the pavement. They are accused of being dirty and spreading diseases. But do they? Why do they come in so many colour variations? And how come we never see baby pigeons?

In terms of their propensity for spreading disease, you would be forgiven for thinking that Feral Pigeons harboured every ailment known to man, plus a few that we perhaps don't yet know about. This is seemingly visually corroborated by the sight of some individuals sporting gammy legs, club feet and very dishevelled plumages. Pigeons are known to carry lurgies like chlamydiosis or psittacosis, a bacterial infection that has flu-like symptoms. The jury is still out as to how much of a health risk they pose to humans, as many experts believe that the chances of catching anything from them are minimal. It is the droppings that we really have to worry about. Fresh droppings plopped on your head, whilst being unpleasant and, contrastingly, a sign of good luck, pose no risk to health. It is when they become dried that things can get dodgy. Spores from these droppings can be carried on the wind and be inhaled as dust. This can cause a flu-like illness in healthy people and a much more serious reaction in those with low immunity. Additionally, accumulations of droppings, which are highly acidic, can cause long-term damage to buildings, much to the chagrin of council officials.

When domesticated animals become feral and return to the wild they normally revert back to their original ancestor's coloration. Feral Pigeons hail from coast-dwelling Rock Doves that, to the untrained eye, look like a normal pigeon. A closer examination would reveal that these truly wild birds all have a similar plumage – the classic pigeon grey with a couple of black wing bars and a white rump patch. In the case of the Feral Pigeon, however, no two birds look the same. If you took a stroll out into your local high street you may see some pigeons that look like classic 'Rock Doves' but with no or variable amounts of white on the rumps.

There are people out there who absolutely love pigeons – to the extent that they devote their waking lives to studying them. One such guy is zoologist Adam Rogers, who has been

FERAL PIGEONS

Squab

A mixed couple

Chequered form

Blue barred form

Pied form

doing some very interesting work with the birds. He has broken pigeons down into three main types. Broadly speaking there is a 'blue barred' type, which is most similar to the wild Rock Dove having two black stripes on its folded wing; a 'chequered' type, which is usually dark with irregular black blotches on its wings and back; and a rarer 'pied' type, which has a mixed genetic heritage and often has a white head and wingtips. Interestingly, Adam has found that pigeons prefer to mate with a bird that looks very different from itself – which keeps the variety of plumages in the population going. Choosing a mate that is genetically different from itself also has the advantage of bolstering the health of its chicks. The ability actively to seek such mates seems to show that pigeons have a remarkable sense of self-awareness – they know what they look like; an attribute that only a few other animals, such as Chimpanzees and dolphins, have. Although Feral Pigeons are renowned for being prolific breeders, research as shown that only the 'chequered' type is capable of breeding during the depths of winter. So it stands to reason that the 'chequered' variety of Feral Pigeon is the most numerous colour form of this ubiquitous species.

Far from being boring and not very intelligent, Feral Pigeons have a fascinating life history, one part of which often flummoxes members of the public – the often-posed question "how come we never see baby pigeons?" The answer is actually quite simple. Young pigeons, or squabs, remain in the nest until they are about the same size as an adult – so when they make their debut appearances on our streets they are often indistinguishable from their parents.

Ring-necked (or Rose-ringed) Parakeets are now fairly well known to urbanites based in southern England, particularly in and around London. And as their range is expanding rapidly across the land, they are also becoming better known farther north. This is a

Feral Pigeons

Ring-necked Parakeets

gregarious and garrulous bird whose native distribution takes in most of India and parts of West Africa. I make no secret of the fact that I am not their greatest fan. They are noisy, numerous and bullies at the bird table. I first noticed them in the late 1970s when I would see the occasional bird fly past me in west London on its way to some unknown destination. At first I disregarded them as being no different from seeing an escaped African Grey Parrot or a Budgie. Over the next 20 years, more and more people began reporting escaped parrots happily feeding at their bird tables. News later broke about a huge roost, which had started from humble beginnings, in the poplars around the Esher Rugby Club ground in Surrey. Some 7,000 birds were gathering each evening, raucously proclaiming their presence from the tops of the trees. This resulted in quite a lot of media attention and plenty of people travelled to witness the spectacle. There were other smaller roosts within south-west London and when the Esher roost site was disturbed due to tree surgery the birds simply moved elsewhere. I would never have guessed that by 2010 my local patch, Wormwood Scrubs, would be playing host to a roost of up to 5,000 birds, drowning out the springtime dawn chorus to which I had become so accustomed.

Questions were being asked as to the provenance of these parakeets and rumours were soon rife. The most popular myth was that they escaped from the set at Shepperton Studios in 1950 where The African Queen, starring Humphrey Bogart and Katharine Hepburn, was being shot. In reality, though, this film was actually shot farther north at the Isleworth Studios. Another story concerned a plane that was flying over south-west London when part of the fuselage fell off; this landed on an aviary and resulted in the birds escaping. Another myth involves a couple who were having a row at home in south-west London. The husband was a keen aviculturist and, out of spite, his good lady left the door of the aviary open allowing the birds to escape. However, my favourite myth as to how the parakeets came to be so prevalent in London concerns the late, great Jimi Hendrix. Legend has it that Jimi stood on Carnaby Street with Adam in one hand and Eve in the other (a male and a female parakeet). He released them, and 40 years later there are 30,000 parakeets at large in the capital.

Despite these various rumours, the real answer to the origin of Britain's Ring-necked Parakeets could not be more unglamorously boring: they are simply escaped pets. Furthermore, the first breeding record in the UK was in fact in the 1850s, in Great Yarmouth. These birds were popular with sailors who kept them as pets – and whenever they docked the birds were able to jump ship. There was even a thriving colony in north Kent during the late 1800s. Despite looking highly tropical in their bright green plumage – and let's face it, when you think parrot you think steamy jungle – Ring-necked Parakeets are hardy birds, part of their range extending to 4,000 feet up in the Himalayas. They are therefore clearly well able to cope with the cold. Added to this, the good old British public love to provide them with excellent bird table cuisine. So, unless things change radically, the Ring-necked Parakeet looks set to become a permanent feature of our towns and cities.

One of the earliest birds to eke out a living on our streets was the humble House Sparrow, having followed us out of our shared ancestral home in Africa and spread across Europe in association with Neolithic farmers. Now, after the farmyard chicken, it is the most widely distributed bird in the world, found on all the continents bar Antarctica. House Sparrows have literally been living by our side for thousands of years, feeding on our spilt grain and discarded scraps, and it is hard to believe that there were probably none in Britain before the arrival of the first humans. It is equally hard to believe that the UK population of this familiar bird fell by 71% between 1971 and 2008. The reason for this decline is a matter of some conjecture, but seems likely to be due to a combination of factors, including the effects of pollution and poor nutrition. Although many other species of birds have also taken to living alongside us, readily accepting the food that we provide in various ways, nesting in man-made structures or roosting next to where we are unconsciously pumping warm air into the atmosphere, they also have viable populations living out in the sticks that have existed there for aeons.

A classic urban bird of old was the Red Kite. This large master of the skies is currently enjoying a renaissance in the UK, thanks to a spate of several very successful reintroduction schemes undertaken since the late 1980s. Prior to this, it had become a rare species in

House Sparrow

Red Kites

Britain, with the nucleus of our by then tiny population centred on mid-Wales. Indeed, the Welsh population was on its knees during the early 1900s, when it dropped to an all-time low of an estimated five pairs. I remember in the early 1980s being one of the many birders who made the annual pilgrimage into deepest Wales just to catch sight of a Red Kite or two to tick off on my year-list.

This journey was akin to the trips that birders still make to this day to the highlands and islands of Scotland to see the avian specialties that only these localities can provide. Birds like Capercaillie, Ptarmigan and Golden Eagle spring to mind. Nowadays, you are equally likely to see Red Kites soaring over the rolling hills and motorways of the Chilterns or Gateshead as drifting across the mountainsides and valleys of Wales. Historically, this was inherently a medieval town bird, swooping over the streets and grabbing any tidbits that could be found. Red Kites were apparently very common in London, where they hung out in flocks. They were also brazen, often stealing food from peoples' hands, and regularly dropped down to pick floating scraps from the surface of the Thames. These kites also had a penchant for stealing bits of clothing and other strange items to adorn their nests, as in fact they still do today.

During the 16th century, the capital's Red Kite population was afforded protected status due to the birds' services to refuse disposal. However, as our towns and cities became more sanitized the kites began to find less food on the streets. This, coupled with the increase in game bird rearing, and the associated persecution of all birds of prey, resulted in the demise of the Red Kite – which, being so obvious, was the first to feel the wrath of man. They lost their protected status and were instead billed as vermin. Fast-forward to today, and the Red Kite news is good. They are making a comeback and are increasingly being seen in urban areas. Although they are still scarce visitors to London and will probably never attain the numbers that once occurred there, keep looking up wherever you may live as you might just see one floating gracefully overhead.

Herring Gull

Herring Gulls are another great example of a species that has taken advantage of the potentially better life that our towns and cities have to offer. They are essentially a coastal bird that is very much ingrained in our culture and folklore. There is no doubt, though, that Herring Gulls polarize opinion. Some of us see them as ice-cream-nicking monsters, whilst others laud them for their beauty and grace. They were and still are the archetypal seaside bird: the seagull. Then something happened. Herring Gulls and their close relative the Lesser Black-backed Gull started to nest within West Country towns in the 1920s, lured in by the availability of easy food – perhaps 40 years prior to the first gulls starting to infiltrate our urban centres. Being smart birds they proliferated and have become very successful. It is this success that has brought them detractors. Some folk lament the existence of these urbanized gulls and, in particular, the ones that chose to raise their raucous families on the low-rise rooftops of city shopping centres like Bristol, Gloucester and Cardiff. The residents who are unfortunate enough to live within a wing flap of a colony often have to contend with having their cars and, worst still, themselves festooned with the acrid droppings produced, and seemingly liberally scatter-gunned, by territorial dive-bombing birds. Of course, you would have to be pretty unlucky to receive such a splattering and would usually have to be invading their rooftop territories to receive such attention.

Every year during the breeding season there is a feeding frenzy amongst Britain's tabloid press, demonizing gulls as wanton, aggressive attackers of defenceless people. And every year conservationists jump to the birds' defence. The truth is that actual strikes against humans are very rare. No gull in its right mind would put itself in danger by attacking someone; if it were to get injured, that would be game over, as the bird would no longer be able to feed and defend itself effectively. Nonetheless, any bad press makes it hard to explain to disgruntled citizens that the two species involved are actually of conservation concern as they are declining nationally at an alarming rate. You might not think it, but the gulls that still live in their classic coastal environment have suffered a severe decrease in numbers, largely due to the depletion of fish stocks.

People are now saying that these large gulls have lost their taste for salt water and bracing sea air, and have instead taken to life on the streets. And I have seen many a newspaper article upholding that claim. Well, it is a complete fallacy, as gulls are great wanderers, some travelling from the far extremities of northern and eastern Europe, and sometimes beyond, just to spend the winter enjoying the delicacies barely hidden within our rubbish dumps.

Just about any bird species found in Britain, whether a resident, regular migrant or rare vagrant, can turn up in an urban area. I have seen Puffins lolling incongruously among flocks of Mallards on the river Thames, and on one memorable occasion a Cory's Shearwater – a rare seabird from the Atlantic – was discovered flying over Regents Park in central London having been forced inland by horrendous weather out at sea. Sometimes it's also possible to see moorland specialists like Red Grouse sitting on rocky watch-points within the outskirts of Bradford. Transatlantic vagrants such as American Robins have occasionally turned up in urban gardens, and Eastern Asian gems like Yellow-browed Warblers have graced wintry inner city bushes – far from the Thai forests where most of their kin spend the winter. In fact, surprisingly few of the 608 bird species recorded in Britain up until the end of 2017 have not occurred in an urban area.

Urban bird research has thrown up another major discovery: the fact that birds have louder songs in city environments than their country counterparts. The purpose of song is mainly two-fold: to establish territories and to attract mates. Cities can be very noisy places and birds have had to adapt and sing louder to be heard over the hubbub. If you are

Red Grouse on the moors above Bradford, West Yorkshire

naturally quiet then a noisy city could prove to be your undoing. The Great Tit's "*teacher-teacher*" song is fairly loud at the best of times, but it has been found that urban birds have developed a higher-pitched song to be heard over the din of traffic. The fascinating thing is that scientists at Aberystwyth University have shown that rural Great Tits were confused by the urban version of their song, while the city birds did not understand the lower rural pitch. It begs the question: is this gradual split in the vocalizations a universal thing amongst urban birds and, if so, does it mean that urban populations of various species will eventually evolve into new species?

Bring on the curious case of San Diego's urban Dark-eyed Juncos. This attractive sparrow-like bird is found right across North America and over time has evolved into several distinct races. The population in the San Diego region on the west coast, which belongs to the Oregon race, breeds 60 miles to the east of the city on Mount Laguna – which happens to be on the southern edge of the Oregon Junco's fairly extensive range. This race is not known as an urban bird, preferring to live its life away from human habitation. However, winter in the mountains is a pretty harsh affair and at this time of year most of the population moves to the lowlands and westwards towards the coast and San Diego, returning in the spring.

But in the early 1980s something changed: a few Oregon Juncos decided not to return to the mountains and instead spent the summer breeding along the coast around San Diego, including in the University of California campus. This community of birds, in the heart of a very urban area, quickly became an isolated outpost of the main Oregon Junco population. It attracted the attentions of scientists who soon got to work studying

Cory's Shearwater

Oregon Junco

this unusual disjunct population. The campus birds were finding plenty of food, ranging from crumbs dropped by lunching students to the natural bounty of insects that was to be found all-year round, attracted to the numerous flower beds. Up in the mountains the foraging is a little more difficult and subject to weather conditions. The scientists discovered that the hot summers on Mount Laguna meant that the birds were restricted to raising just one brood, usually between May and June. Meanwhile, down on the coastal campus, the birds were raising up to four broods a year and nesting from late February through to the end of August.

The increase in family duties saw a change in the birds' behaviour, with the males helping to rear the young – something that did not happen up in the mountains. Instead of the usual territorial behaviour displayed by the Mount Laguna birds, the campus males' white outer tail feathers and black heads (both used in threat displays) became more diffuse and less intense and, crucially, the birds were less aggressive towards each other. As well as this, their average wing length was reduced and the tone of their song changed, becoming higher pitched and more audible over the constant low rumble of traffic. They also developed a different attitude towards people: whereas the mountain birds were wary, the campus birds became almost blasé towards folk. The scientists set up an aviary and introduced a few captured campus birds as well as a few from Mount Laguna. The birds were subject to the same light, diet and living conditions. It soon became apparent that the two populations did not really mix and retained their separate characteristics. The experiment highlighted that the evolution shown by the campus birds over 30 years was genetic and not just due to the environment. Evolution, it seems, is not something that always happens over millennia. It happens every day.

Finally, as an urban birder you will sometimes bump into birds that despite looking comfortable in their environment are as alien as you can get. These are birds that have invariably escaped from a collection or out of someone's house. During my time I have been confused by an array of tropical finches, parrots and a panoply of waterfowl while out urban birding. I'm often asked whether these birds are able to survive in the wild here in Britain. Well, a lot of the smaller, more 'tropical' species don't due to their special dietary requirements or, as they stick out like sore thumbs, because they fall easy prey to predators.

I once discovered a bright yellow Budgie amongst a Goldfinch flock on my local patch. It looked totally out of place as well as totally visible. I was surprised to see it for four days on the trot, feeding with the Goldfinches, but by the fifth day it had disappeared, despite the continued presence of its erstwhile flock mates. No doubt it provided a tasty snack for the resident Sparrowhawk. Amazingly, the Budgerigar did once have a toehold in the UK when a small flock managed to survive in the wild for many years on the Isles of Scilly.

Some parrot species have been a bit more successful in acclimatizing to city life. Aside from the aforementioned Ring-necked Parakeets, Britain also pays host to the small green-and-grey Monk Parakeet from South America, which holds the distinction of being the only parrot in the world to build its own nest. The problem is that these birds breed colonially and can build communal nests the size and weight of a small car on top of flimsy structures like telegraph poles. The nests are like apartment blocks with each pair having its own entrance. Imagine such constructions in the streets of Edinburgh or Manchester – it just would not work. The main concern over these birds is the possible negative impact on fruit farms if they were to become established. Indeed, in its native Argentina this parrot is regarded as an agricultural pest. So, in the UK the decision was taken by the Department for Environment, Food and Rural Affairs (defra) to wipe out the fledgling populations in Borehamwood in Hertfordshire and Mudshute Farm in east London before they had a chance to really establish themselves. The eradication programme has been largely successful, although not all conservationists were in agreement with the decision to carry it out.

Monk Parakeet

WHAT IS THAT BIRD?

This may seem like a stupid question but in truth there is no such thing as a stupid question in the world of natural history. By my reckoning, every question leads to further knowledge. I still ask a truckload of questions when I am out birding. Some are very basic and are either addressed to myself when I am on my own, or directed to whomever I am with at the time – whether they are an expert or not.

I remember birding at a reservoir in Aberdeen with the Chairman of the local RSPB Members Group who was a regionally renowned birder with a lot of experience. We came across a cluster of Common Gulls loafing on a raft in the middle of the reservoir. Superficially similar to a Herring Gull, these gulls are usually recognizable by their smaller size, greenish legs and a slim yellowish bill. Whilst quietly scanning through the group I came across a younger-looking bird that seemed to have pinkish legs. I was stumped and did not have my field guide with me either. Was the bird a Common Gull or something far rarer? So I posed the question thinking that my companion would instantly know the answer. He didn't. In fact, he was happy that I had mentioned it as he was thinking just the same thing. When we got back to his home we pored through the identification books and worked out that it was indeed an immature Common Gull. They have pink legs for the first couple of years of life before they turn greenish. Nothing ventured, nothing learned.

Black-headed Gull

Never be afraid of asking what you may deem as a silly question, because it won't be. So, back to the original question: what is a bird? Although most of the world's birds look like birds, in that they are feathered, have beaks and possess wings that they use to transport themselves through the air, some families look nothing like your classic sparrow – penguins being a good example. Over the years, friends have often quite seriously asked me whether penguins are birds or not. It may sound funny but imagine you are an alien from Planet Zorgo and had just crash-landed on Antarctica. The first thing that you clap eyes on is an Emperor Penguin squatting on some remote frozen ice floe. Understandably, you would probably struggle to realize that you were looking at a bird. Rest assured that despite the fact that I continually bang on about anything turning up anywhere at anytime, I can categorically state that you will not be seeing a wild penguin in a UK city anytime soon. Penguins are distinctly un-urban and, besides, are residents of the Southern Hemisphere, where they generally shun residential areas. That said, I recently did try to twitch a blind Humboldt Penguin, one of those small, stripy black-and-white species that is so popular in zoos. It was hanging out in a wetland on the outskirts of Lima, Peru. Quite why it was blind and, crucially, how it was managing to survive was the $64,000 question. Needless to say, I was unsuccessful in my twitching quest – I didn't see it and it certainly didn't see me!

Birds are warm-blooded creatures belonging to the class of living things called Aves. They are most obviously characterized by the fact that they are covered in feathers, have wings and a 'toothless' beak (or, perhaps more correctly, bill), and lay eggs. There are around 10,500 species worldwide depending on what authority you consult, subdivided into orders and families, with members ranging in size from the Ostrich down to the minute and the now sadly rather rare Bee Hummingbird. I could go on, but I guess you already know the basics about what makes a bird a bird. So how does this knowledge help you in your daily urban birding?

Pick up any field guide and you will discover in the introductory pages drawings depicting the topography of a bird. In other words, the composite parts on the outside that are visible to us. There will be a confusing array of pointers highlighting the names of various tracts of feathers like the primaries, secondaries and undertail coverts. In addition, certain characteristic features that may be useful for identification will also be highlighted – such as supercilium, wingbars and hind claws. These details may mean little to a beginner birder but to the more experienced watcher are the standardized terminology used when describing birds for the purpose of confirming their identification. But even seasoned birders struggle to remember all of the terms used. I am frequently getting my tertials mixed up with my secondary coverts and usually give up when it comes to counting the individual primary feathers on gulls.

At this stage in the game it's not necessary to know anything about the minutiae of feather detail, but simply to become familiar with a few key parts. The secret to identifying birds is all about watching them. To start with, try to pay particular attention to just six sections of the bird that you are watching: its head, back, wings, tail, underparts and bare parts (bill and legs). There are other pointers to look out for, such as calls and behaviour, but for the sake of simplicity I will deal with those a little later.

When confronted with a strange bird, initially try to note down the general colours and plumage patterns. Is it streaked or are there one or two main colours involved? Did you

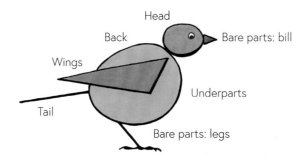

get a chance to notice the colour of its bill or legs? The other element to consider is size. Just how big is that bird in comparison with another that you are familiar with nearby, such as a Starling or the larger Blackbird? For me, it is all about familiarity. By getting intimate with the common birds in your neighbourhood you will come to notice that they are of varying size. A Blue Tit is bigger than a Wren but clearly smaller than a House Sparrow. The chain links will continue until you get to the other end of the scale and make the connection that a Canada Goose is smaller than a Mute Swan. Armed with that information, if you see a bird in the company of other species then you will be able to say with some confidence that the streaky brown bird that you saw was bigger than a sparrow though smaller than a Starling. This will help to narrow down your search through the field guide. Making very basic notes forces you to look at the various parts of a bird and makes it easier to then match your 'mystery' bird with those illustrated in your field guide or bird app.

I have suggested that you should look at six areas on a bird that you are trying to recognize. That may sound like a lot of things to look out for, and perhaps it is at first, but as you get used to looking at birds more quizzically you will be surprised how quickly your brain will train itself to see these pointers. So, let's pretend that you are seeing a Blue Tit for the first time in your life. Once you get over the sheer glee of seeing something new, how would you best describe it in order to achieve the correct identity?

▶ **Head:** blue cap, black throat, black line around face, black line running through eye that starts at the bill and ends by joining the black border around face; rest of face white.

▶ **Back:** greenish.

▶ **Wings:** blue with a white stripe.

▶ **Tail:** blue.

▶ **Underparts:** yellow.

▶ **Bare parts:** bill and legs blackish.

Piecing these notes together will build a picture that could only fit a Blue Tit's profile. There are very few birds in Britain that even vaguely have that colour combination. The Blue Tit's small size will tell you that it is not a Grey Wagtail, which despite having a yellow belly has a long tail, a grey-blue back and behaves very differently.

Helpfully, there are field guides out there in which the birds are arranged within their pages by colour grouping as opposed to a strictly scientific classification. If you feel that a book like that would be helpful to you, then you should go ahead and get one. Although you may feel slightly embarrassed when you discover that the bird you have written notes on is very common and obvious, do not despair. Even experienced birders would struggle to draw the shape and extent of a Robin's red breast from memory. It is by continually looking at birds that you begin to log the overall look and feel of the regular species you come across and are thus able to identify them without much thought. You may never be able to remember the shape of a Robin's red breast but you will still be able to recognize a Robin instantly if it hopped onto your windowsill. Never get bogged down with the finer detail of a bird's plumage: look instead at a bird in its entirety, taking into account its overall appearance.

By simplifying everything you will be able to describe a strange bird in simple language without having to use technical terms. It is all about getting used to the general look and shape of a bird by gently training yourself to clock certain plumage and body shape details automatically, especially when you just get a fleeting glimpse. Try not to concentrate on just one plumage detail but rather the 'jizz' of a bird. Far from being rude, jizz is a term used by birders to describe the overall impression or appearance of a bird. Remember, not all birds will sit up in the open to allow us the pleasure of prolonged views. I touched on this earlier, but the other thing to make a note of is the bird's behaviour. Was it furtively foraging in the branches of a tree? Was it walking on the ground or did it hop? Was it flicking its wings or wagging its tail?

Why not practise making notes on the behaviour of the birds you recognize that come into your garden. Even if they are only mental notes you will soon discover that some species have distinct behavioural traits that are effectively species-specific signatures. For example, when a Blackbird swoops past and lands on a tree it will then slowly raise and lower its tail. No other thrush does this, and that is how I often pick out its similar-looking but much scarcer congener, the Ring Ouzel. Even if I only see the latter's dark plumage rather than its diagnostic white gorget, the fact that it did not raise its tail tells me instantly that it is not a Blackbird.

Could you draw a Robin's red breast from memory?

Don't worry if you're not able to pick up every feature on a bird, as you will rarely need all of them to identify it successfully. Obviously, the more you can recollect the better, but bear in mind that some of the key features mentioned in the books may not necessarily be that obvious in real-life situations. In the case of male Blackbirds, I often overlook the fact that they have a distinctive, yellow eye-ring, but they are still clearly Blackbirds. If you look closely you may notice that your Blackbird is browner rather than black – in which case you can tell that it is either an adult female or a youngster. And, if you look very closely, you may see that the bill colours of the Blackbirds in your garden vary too, an indication of a bird's age. Some Blackbirds may even have some white feathers, a sign of albinism. But there is a lot of individual variation and it can be very confusing. The important thing is not to be concerned if you did not notice all these differences straight away. This kind of attention to detail tends to come gradually as you really begin to watch and study birds.

To this day, I am still noticing new details on even our most common birds that I have watched literally for decades. A good example would be the Sparrowhawk. It was many years before I noticed the two whitish spots that they have at the back of their head that seemingly imitate a pair of eyes. I have mentioned the Blackbird as a species to practise describing, but not all species are as simple and obvious as a male Blackbird, and most are a little more complicated to describe. What about a Dunnock with its hues of brown and grey, or the gaudy Jay? This may all sound totally overwhelming but I can assure you that it will only seem like that in the beginning. Eventually, you will be looking at birds in a completely different way. You will subconsciously scan them to register their salient identification features, as well as watching out for any interesting displays of behaviour. It will become second nature the more you practise describing a bird. Just keep things very simple to begin with.

A big part of birding involves seeing birds that just defy identification. It may be as a result of a fleeting glance in bad light, but could be an individual displaying anomalous plumage, an escaped captive bird that is not found naturally in the UK or a genuine rarity not featured in your field guide. Be prepared to let some birds remain unidentified – just let them go. Don't feel pressured to put a name to everything that crosses your path and bear in mind the fact that even the experts cannot identify everything they see. Some groups of birds, like immature gulls, warblers, pipits and waders, perplex the most experienced birders as they can be really troublesome to identify.

Part of the allure of birds is that they are not silent. Life would not be the same without hearing the various calls and songs around us, even if they are simply relegated to just being part of the background soundtrack of urban life. Some calls are distinctive, such as a crow's caw or a gull's yelp. They are universal sounds, variations of which are to be heard in countless towns and cities throughout the world. Whenever I take city folk on walks around their neighbourhoods I am always surprised that the noises I take for granted often go unheard to the untrained ear. Once you really start to watch birds you will begin to hear sounds emanating from tiny throats that you never expected – and that is where the confusion really starts. Bird calls and songs take time to master and some of the summer visiting migrants only sing for a short period of time, often not long enough to give you the opportunity to get to know them well.

Some species groups have similar songs and take time and experience to differentiate. The songs of Blackcaps and Garden Warblers or Sedge and Reed Warblers, for example, are

Blackbird (female showing some white feathers)

Meadow Pipits are the archetypal 'little brown job'.

very similar and can be tough to sort out. To add to the confusion, some birds have weird calls that are rarely uttered and yet others, such as Bullfinches and Jays, have songs that practically no one ever hears. The best way to familiarize yourself with the countless different calls and songs is to hear them in the field and to try to find the musician responsible. Begin to associate the sound with the bird you have seen and when you hear it in the future you will know that the "*pink-pink*" call coming from a nearby tree is indeed a Chaffinch. Listening to bird calls and songs on your smartphone, tablet or computer is another good way to learn, if a little prescriptive. But there really is no substitute for hearing birds in their proper environment – out in nature. As with general bird identification, do not beat yourself up if you are finding it difficult to remember calls. There is no national level of knowledge to achieve, no exam to pass. Just learn at your own pace. You will never know all the calls that birds make. No one does.

If you try to describe any strange bird you see by breaking it down into these simple components – size, shape, colours and patterns, calls and song, and behaviour – then your urban birding life will instantly begin to get a little easier. The Blackbirds in my garden were the first birds that I really studied and got to grips with, even though I wasn't aware of it at the time. To start with I noticed that there was a difference between the males and females, and then I moved on to telling these birds apart from the other species that were around. They were clearly bigger and bulkier than the similarly hued Starlings, and I also noticed that their carriage and behaviour was different. I soon realized that they made a range of distinctive noises too – ranging from that beautiful, fluty full song to a harsh, chattering alarm call. As a beginner it took me quite some time and effort to register the Blackbird's jizz in my brain – but it was a very pleasurable learning curve and I learnt a lot about the birds visiting my garden in the process. So, if you're patient and persevere with studying the common birds you come across, you'll be surprised how quickly you can recognize them, even with the briefest of views.

Blackbird

Grey Heron

THE BIRDS IN YOUR NEIGHBOURHOOD

It is a commonly held belief that Robins only come into our gardens during the winter, and especially when it's snowing. I discovered this popular misconception whilst conducting my recent campaign to find Britain's National Bird. Even some of the supposedly educated folk in the media that I came into contact with firmly believed that Robins largely disappeared during the summer months. I totally get it though: if you are unfamiliar with bird life per se then you will not know much about the avian goings on in a British town or city. The truth is that there is considerable flux when it comes to the populations of birds throughout the year.

Seasons

Birds and their behaviour are influenced by the seasons. Classically, springtime is the time of awakening. Plants start to flower and trees come into bloom. Insect life explodes and many birds become engaged in courtship, nest-building and egg-laying. Summer-visiting species like Common Terns and House Martins start to arrive, either passing through to more suitable breeding areas or actually taking up territories amongst the more resident birds. Late spring and early summer is also the best time to witness the aural delight of the dawn chorus. This cacophony of sound in which males of several species individually proclaim their territories in song is best experienced just before dawn within an area of woodland. It is a phenomenon that, at its height, only lasts for a few short weeks. However, even if you are an inner city dweller you do not have to miss out if you can't get to a nearby wood. A watered-down performance involving fewer species can still be enjoyed right within the heart of our cities – provided you are prepared to get up early before the traffic din starts!

House Martin (juvenile)

Swallow

During the height of the summer, breeding is in full swing. This is the time when many species become quieter and less easy to see. They are busy raising young and trying not to draw attention to themselves, although this is often not helped by the incessant begging calls of their youngsters. Late summer, when the last of the broods have fledged and young birds are learning to cope for themselves, things become even quieter as the adults start their moult (replace their feathers). It is at this stage that they are most vulnerable to predation and many become much more skulking. So much so, in fact, that many people think that their Blackbirds and Robins have disappeared. As summer melds into autumn, most birds have completed their moult and have either migrated or, in the case of tits and thrushes, begun to form roving flocks looking for food. Our remaining birds are joined by passage migrants moving through from farther north and east, and the first of the winter visitors such as the Redwing also arrive in their midst. Winter has historically been thought of as the season when there is little movement. This is true to a degree but if there is hard weather farther north it encourages more birds to move southwards.

Be aware that the old urban birding adage is always at play: anything can turn up anywhere at anytime. Sometimes, birds that we associate with a particular season may linger and become unusual sightings. Swallows have been seen into November and classic winter birds such as the Goldeneye, an attractive northern European diving duck, can swim around in urban areas even in mid-summer – like the one I once saw on the Manchester Ship Canal. To add to the complexity, with some species that we tend to consider as residents there are often sub-populations that partake in annual migrations. Our Blackbirds, for example, are joined by many thousands of their Nordic cousins every winter. These are slightly longer-winged (although in reality this is tough to discern in the field), and are often shyer and more furtive than our resident birds.

Migration

Birds move around for a variety of reasons. Sometimes it is just about juveniles generally dispersing to other areas. But certain species, particularly in northern and eastern Europe and beyond, are nomadic in their movements. They can suddenly show up in an area one year, and even breed, but then completely disappear the next. This movement may be triggered by the lack of available food in their natal areas. If food is really scarce, possibly precipitated by a good breeding season that results in a significant population increase, an irruption could occur. The archetypal irruption species is that Christmas pin-up, the Waxwing. Small numbers occur here in most years, but every now and again massive numbers turn up in Britain, initially making landfall in eastern Scotland and then spreading out across the rest of the country.

Of course, quite a number of the birds that we are familiar with, such as Swallows and Turtle Doves, undertake full-on migrations, with the entire population shifting from one region to another, often on a broad front. There are also altitudinal migrants that leave their breeding grounds in higher areas to winter in the more temperate lowlands, although there are relatively few birds in the UK that fall into this category. Partial migration is when some populations of birds, like the Blackbirds I mentioned previously, migrate, whereas other members of the same species stay put. Migration is indeed a complex subject, and certainly

Waxwings

Turtle Dove

Starling

Goldcrests are often the main component of coastal autumnal falls.

not an exact science – but what we do know is that we don't know an enormous amount about it. That said, scientists are gradually unravelling the secrets of migration through ringing studies and, latterly, the use of geo-tags to gather information about the journeys birds undertake.

But what is migration actually all about, and can we witness it during our urban lives? The answer to the last point is an emphatic *Yes*, as it not just confined to coastal headlands and famous nature reserves, but happens across huge swathes of the country.

Many smaller birds and waders migrate at night as this reduces the potential for predation, setting off at sunset having spent the previous daylight hours feeding and resting. It is also usually cooler at night with more settled atmospheric conditions. They will often continue this strategy of moving on night after night until they reach their destination. You can sometimes notice this phenomenon by the sudden presence of a range of different species in your garden or an increase in the number of individual birds. It explains why one morning you may peer outside or visit your patch and see next to nothing, yet the following morning find the place bouncing with birds. It's important to remember that not all migrants are the obvious species such as Cuckoos: the Robins, Dunnocks, Great Tits and Starlings you see may, in fact, have emanated from Eastern Europe. You may also notice the sudden appearance, then disappearance, of birds like Swallows and Swifts. They are just passing through, feeding along the way – a survival technique that avoids wasting time lingering in one spot during migration.

Other birds, particularly larger ones such as migrating raptors, are diurnal, travelling during the day by using the thermals that only occur when the sun is up. Raptors are often dependent upon the uplift of thermals to carry them over potentially hazardous sea crossings, avoiding the need to expend excessive energy. But, interestingly, some birds of prey, such as falcons, Ospreys and harriers, are not restricted by the need for thermals and seem quite happy flapping in steady flight over short sea crossings and over land.

So, where can you watch migration in urban areas? Well, the answer is practically anywhere. However, do not expect phenomenal movements of birds swarming into your area, as evidence of migration is usually a subtle thing. Remember, most migratory journeys occur out of sight, either way above your head and beyond your vision or during the dead of night. Spring migration is particularly hard to witness as a spectacle because in many species males race to arrive on their breeding grounds before the females to claim a territory. In the autumn, there are far more birds on the move because we now have masses of juveniles in the mix as well. Some species, such as Swallows, gather in large numbers at favoured spots to refuel before moving on together. You are therefore more likely to see groups of birds on the move at this time of year.

If I wander around my local patch in the spring and notice a few migrant species in ones and twos then I'm having a good day. However, on rare occasions I have been fortunate enough to experience a 'fall' – when larger numbers of migrating birds than normal are brought down,

'Vis migging' from Tower 42, London

Migrating Wood Pigeons

usually by inclement weather. Such events tend to be by the coast where migrants make their first landfall. There are some amazing stories of thousands of birds being found by bewildered birders the morning after a night of severe weather. Tales of coastal bushes dripping with exhausted birds is etched into ornithological folklore. News of such falls normally has keen birders lacing up their boots and rushing over to the scene to sift through the common migrants for signs of something rarer in their midst. It is one of those phenomena that every birder would love to experience at least once in their birding lifetime.

Falls involving birds in urban areas are a rare event unless you happen to live by the coast, as, following landfall, migrating flocks gradually move inland and dissipate. I have, however, had some exceptional experiences at my local patch in London when I have discovered unusually high numbers of a migrant that I would normally only record in ones or twos. There is often advance warning of such an event when very high numbers of migrants are recorded at traditional coastal spots. For instance, several springs ago, after hearing about large falls of spring migrants on the south coast, a few days later I found no less than 11 Spotted Flycatchers on my patch. They were hunting insects in a loose flock on a stretch of embankment barely a hundred yards long. More recently, an incredible 12 Redstarts and upwards of 40 Wheatears were present on my patch in a clear window during a period of foul weather that held up migrating birds in northern France.

Visible migration watching, or 'vis migging' as it is often referred to by keen birders, has become a very popular pastime. It is usually conducted by standing at a vantage point, like a coastal headland or on top of high ground, in the path of a well-known migration route. Observers arrive predawn and if the weather is favourable could be treated to a continual stream of birds passing overhead.

There has always been a small number of urban birders who spend time looking up to notice birds passing over their patches on migration. Indeed, according to the late Eric Simms, wildlife broadcaster, writer and BBC sound recordist, birders used to gather on Parliament Hill in London during the autumn in the 1950s and 60s to watch visible migration. They soon discovered that migrants, regardless of species, regularly followed a route that took them through north London. The birds would often pass by at head height – exciting stuff! But if you visit your patch, sit in the park at lunchtime, or even just look up as you walk down the high street, you will have every chance of seeing a party of Swallows swoop through or a flock of finches passing over. And if you can get yourself onto a rooftop you will then have a chance of seeing the migrating flocks at their level. Don't worry if you cannot recognize the species as they fly overhead – just enjoy the spectacle. Often the din of city life drowns out any distinguishing calls, but more usually the birds are too high up or you may see them too late to get identifiable views. Be prepared to spend a couple of hours after first light watching for movement – it will usually happen in fits and starts, so be patient.

Weather

To improve your chances of predicting and seeing migration in action you have to become a bit of an amateur meteorologist. As a result, you may find that your favourite TV programme will quickly become the weather forecast. The squiggly lines and symbols so beloved by the presenters may seem hard to interpret at first, but once you get a general understanding of weather patterns this may dictate the timing of the visits to your patch and other birding locations.

Here are a few pointers:

▶ The squiggly lines that I referred to are isobars that are shaped around weather systems; the closer together the isobars are, the stronger the wind will be.

▶ Anticyclones are often referred to as areas of high pressure in which the winds are generally light and flow clockwise. Under these conditions the air is descending, which inhibits cloud formation. In the summer this often brings fine, warm weather, and in the winter cold, frosty conditions.

▶ The wind direction around a depression, also called a low pressure area or 'low', is anticlockwise. The air within rises and cools, and water vapour condenses to form clouds and perhaps precipitation. Consequently, the weather is often cloudy, wet and windy.

▶ The term 'weather front' is used for four different situations, the two most obvious being:

   ▶ cold fronts, the boundary between warm air and cold air, with the denser, colder air replacing the warmer air pushing underneath it. In these conditions, the wind often picks up and rain normally occurs in association; and

   ▶ warm fronts, which are essentially the opposite and often bring a gradual increase in rainfall as the front approaches, followed by a general warming after the front passes.

On the weather map, the weather fronts are symbolized by triangles (cold front) and/or half circles (warm front) situated on the isobars themselves.

An important point to remember is that any depiction of weather on a map reflects a frozen moment in time, as high and low pressure systems are mobile. Low pressure emanates from out in the Atlantic and moves across Britain from the south-west to the north-east, sometimes taking less than a day. Highs, on the other hand, often hang around for a while, blocking the movement of low pressure systems.

But what does all this mean to the urban birder? Well, generally speaking, birds need clear skies and a tailwind to help them on their way during migration. In the autumn, travelling conditions are perfect for them when there is an area of high pressure over the UK. Light northerly winds will provide a helpful tailwind for their southward journey and a lack of rain and clear skies is obviously beneficial. The reverse scenario applies in the spring, when a southerly airflow provides the tailwind that aids the birds on their journey north. Bad weather, strong winds and, perversely, no wind can affect migration, with many birds choosing to sit it out until conditions are favourable again. It is when these circumstances occur *en route* that birds drop down into the first area of available cover they encounter.

Recently, I was birding around the streets of Hartlepool Headland in Cleveland and heard incredible stories from the local birders of thousands of autumnal Redwings and Fieldfares pitching down on rooftops and gables, with one small garden lawn having several hundred of these tired thrushes covering the ground. These falls of migrants provide great excitement for us birders. That is why having a basic knowledge of how the weather is looking can help you predict the appearance of migrants on your patch. Nothing really beats the thrill of finding groups of migrating birds in your local urban area, or the excitement of knowing that they can potentially turn up anywhere – even in the middle of the largest city.

Roosts

It may sound perverse, but some birds choose to congregate in the centre of a town or city, sometimes in large communal roosts. Most of the species concerned are essentially solitary or, at most, usually only to be found in small flocks during the day outside of the breeding season. Roosting in numbers and huddling together in close proximity is an efficient way of conserving energy, and in some cases generates sufficient heat to see an individual through the night. Smaller birds like Treecreepers, Long-tailed Tits and Wrens, for example, often bundle together in crevices and nestboxes, clearly to keep warm. Communal roosts also provide some form of protection, as there is always safety in numbers, and many scientists believe they have a social dimension, too. Winter roosting in urban areas has the additional fillip of being warmer than the surrounding countryside due to the heat island effect that I have explained previously.

The key exponents of urban roosting are the Pied Wagtails that flock together to slumber in trees and bushes near to buildings. Starlings also take advantage of our structures for roosting purposes, whilst around cemeteries and in large parks in London thousands of Ring-necked Parakeets have added their raucous voices to the avian nightlife.

Starling roost at Palace Pier, Brighton, East Sussex

Ring-necked Parakeet roost

What birds can you look for?

This is a question that many people ask when embarking on their first urban birding field trips. Well, urban birdlife amounts to more than just the obvious candidates, since anything can turn up anywhere – and often does. There are very few birds that are truly tied to a life in towns and cities, and even those species most often encountered in urban environments are generally also well represented in more rural areas.

Birds move around randomly, as well as seasonally, so over the course of a year the newbie urban birder in Britain will certainly be confronted by many species that don't appear in the guides to garden birds. In spite of the unpredictability that birds clearly display, in this section I have provided a brief summary and description of the 45 species that I think you are most likely to come across. However, it is important to remember that this book was never intended to be a field guide. For example, when describing plumages, I have not confused the issue by covering the various immature plumages that some species show. I guess you could call what follows a sort of 'ready reckoner' of our more familiar urban birds; once you get to grips with these species, noticing other less familiar birds will hopefully become a little easier.

Cormorant in Portsmouth Docks, Hampshire

Mute Swan

Totally unmistakable, this huge white bird has come to epitomize grace and matrimony. They pair for life and hang around a lot as a duo. They also have a very engaging courtship display in which the two birds face each other with necks curved in a gentle 'S'-shape that, with a little imagination on our part, somehow makes the shape of a heart. How lovely.

On the flip side of swan psychology is the blatant aggression that males can sometimes show. They are persistent in chasing off their offspring once they are self-sufficient and deemed to have outstayed their welcome. Swans are also famous for the commitment they show in defending their nests. They have been credited for being able to break arms with a single blow of a mighty wing. Such attacks are thankfully very rare, but if the fear of sparking the ire of an angry male dissuades people from interfering with their nests, then so be it.

Canada Goose

As it says on the tin, this bird is not a native Brit. That said, it is one of the most recognizable birds that you're likely to come across as you take a walk around the lake in your local park. Its large size, brown body and black neck with a white chinstrap makes it easy to identify.

Mallard

This is the archetypal 'duck' so prevalent on almost any stretch of urban water. Mallards are always the first on the scene whenever there are breadcrumbs to be had and often become very tame in the presence of man. This duck really has urban living off to a tee. They have been noted nesting in the strangest of places, even well away from water high up on a balcony of a block of flats. The females are a typical 'duck' brown but the males for most

of the year have a beautiful sheeny bottle-green head and dark mauve chest. The male is brightly plumaged for a reason, and that is to attract a mate. Groups of males can often be seen rowdily chasing a single female, each with only one thing on their mind – procreation. Once she has been fertilized, the male leaves her to incubate and rear the ducklings alone, and swans off to moult. During the summer and into autumn he sheds his gaudy feathers and replaces them with a more dowdy, female-like plumage. During this process he is flightless for part of the time and becomes much more secretive.

Tufted Duck

Another fairly conspicuous member of the urban watery scene, the male's black-and-white garb, complete with wispy tuft, makes him stand out among all the other waterbirds. The females are dull brown but should still be easily recognizable, as this species loves floating and diving out in the open in the middle of lakes and reservoirs. In town and city centres they will readily come to bread thrown to them by members of the public.

Great Crested Grebe

This gorgeous, medium-sized waterbird is a regular fixture of many urban lakes and reservoirs. Although looking like a slim, long-necked and sharp-billed duck, it is in fact not related to the duck tribe at all. Indeed, the grebe family does not seem to have any close relatives, and most scientists now consider penguins to be their closest cousins!

Great Crested Grebes dive after fish and love waterbodies with reedbeds or vegetation-fringed islands. During the breeding season both sexes sport black ear tufts and black-tipped russet head plumes that they use to good effect when courting. Their elegant display involves both birds facing each other on the water amidst much head-wagging and gift-bearing, with ear tufts and ruff splayed. During the winter they lose their colourful head adornments to become largely grey-brown on their upperparts and whitish below.

Moorhen

This Duck-like bird is actually a member of the rail family, and is a common inhabitant of vegetated rivers and canals, and waterbodies ranging in size from small duck ponds to large lakes and reservoirs with natural banks. Although innately a little shy, urban Moorhens often swim or stride out into the open to reveal themselves, especially when a scrum of ducks is scrabbling over scraps that have been provided for them. Seen up-close, they are rather elegant birds with a largely dark blue-grey body and a red facial shield and red bill with a yellow tip. They also have quite long, yellow-green legs with big feet. And if you look carefully, you may notice a red garter at the very top their legs.

Most other members of the rail family are shy denizens of reedbeds and marshlands, and have fairly narrow bodies. Despite appearing to be rather feeble flyers, rails are great wanderers and the Moorhen is no exception, sometimes turning up in the middle of woods miles from any water, or as a surprise garden visitor.

Coot

Most non-birders would regard the Coot as a type of duck, as it behaves in a similar way and is often seen in their company. But it is, in fact, another member of the rail family and closely related to the Moorhen. Its uniform slate-grey plumage is relieved only by a white bill and facial shield, making this bird instantly recognizable.

Coots are found in many of the same habitats as Moorhens but tend to shun small ponds and are more often found on open water, where they can gather in large numbers during the winter. Where they are common, Coots are not averse to competing with the ducks and geese for food scraps thrown in their direction.

Cormorant

The Cormorant is a large, fish-eating 'seabird' and a fairly recent colonist of urban areas, absolutely loving our watercourses and waterbodies. Close up, they are rather reptilian in appearance, with an oily looking black plumage that has a hint of a blue and green sheen, broken only by a white throat and, during the breeding season, white thigh spots.

These birds constantly dive after fish and when not hunting are normally to be seen variously standing on top of gasometers, electricity pylons or trees with their wings open. In flight, they are often mistaken for geese, especially when they fly in a 'V'-formation.

Grey Heron

Colloquially known as a crane amongst some older urban folk, the Grey Heron is very much a feature of almost any inner city watercourse and sometimes even visits gardens, much to the chagrin of pond owners. Its general shape and colour scheme, and patient demeanour whilst fishing, make it unmistakable. In the air, its neck is folded back and it flies with the ponderous action of a large bird of prey. However, the long, trailing legs should put paid to any possible confusion with a wayward and highly unlikely urban eagle.

Kestrel

Once Britain's most common bird of prey, the Kestrel has now been relegated to third place, after the Common Buzzard and the Sparrowhawk. Mostly hunting rodents and large insects, Kestrels can, and often do, turn their talons on small birds. They are usually seen hovering by motorway verges or over open parkland, and are the only small raptor in the UK that habitually hovers.

Sparrowhawk

Originally a woodland predator, this amazing hawk has found its way into our towns and cities and is now a familiar urban citizen. Most of us see Sparrowhawks only fleetingly, usually hurtling through our garden in hot pursuit of a terrified small bird.

Although often mistaken for Kestrels, Sparrowhawks never hover; they are ambush-hunters with a distinctive flap-flap-glide wing action in straight flight. However, they are sometimes seen circling at great height, when their rounded rather than pointed wingtips can be seen.

Peregrine

Truly the king of the urban jungle, the Peregrine is now as expected a part of city natural life as the Feral Pigeons upon which they feed. Large falcons, they power themselves through our city skies on the lookout for prey. They favour prominent perches on top of cranes, buildings and towers to survey their kingdom, often sitting for what seems like ages and appearing like an irregular blob.

Many urban centres have Peregrine Watchpoints set up for members of the public to observe these magnificent raptors through telescopes, under the guidance of local experts. Check to see if there is a watchpoint near to where you live and go and take a look.

Black-headed Gull

The most abundant gull in the UK, this bird, despite its name, has not got a black head. It actually has a brown hood that is replaced during the winter months by a white head with a couple of dark splodges behind its eye. It is the smallest of our common gulls and if you look at the wings of a flying bird you may notice a white stripe along the front edge – a classic sign that you are looking at a

Black-headed Gull. It is most numerous in urban areas during the winter, when our breeding population is augmented by thousands of birds from continental Europe.

Herring Gull

This is the classic, yelping, archetypal seagull. Adults have grey wings with black tips, a white body, pink legs and a yellow bill with a red spot. It is a large bird that is very much a part of our urban lives – you only have to look up in most towns and cities, and you will notice one drifting overhead at some point.

Lesser Black-backed Gull

This is another obvious gull once you get your eye in. Although superficially similar to its close relative the Herring Gull, the wings are slate grey and it has yellow legs. With experience, you may be able to detect the generally slightly slimmer build and deeper voice.

Wood Pigeon

The most common pigeon in the UK, the Wood Pigeon is as likely to be seen waddling the streets in some city centres looking for crumbs as its feral congener. Bigger and chunkier than the Feral Pigeon, it has a diagnostic white patch on the side of the neck and a white crescent on each wing that is obvious in flight.

Feral Pigeon

This totally familiar bird almost warrants no description, although it can be confused with its more common cousin, the Wood Pigeon, and in flight could possibly be mistaken for a falcon. Feral Pigeons come in many different varieties, although most are based on three or four basic plumages (as explained in the *What is an urban bird?* section). Although they are the favoured food of urban Peregrines, it is interesting to note that in level flight a Feral Pigeon can outfly its mortal enemy.

Collared Dove

It is hard to believe that this common and widespread small dove was unknown in the UK prior to 1950. A natural colonist from Asia, it is very much a suburban bird and not often found wandering inner city streets. The Collared Dove is readily identified by its uniform buffy plumage and narrow black half-collar. Like our urban pigeons, it is capable of breeding all-year round and has been known to nest in some pretty weird places.

Great Spotted Woodpecker

This is the most likely of our three resident woodpeckers to be found in urban areas. It is a little smaller than a Blackbird and strikingly black-and-white with red under the tail. Although essentially a woodland bird, preferring areas where stands of large trees provide nesting sites, it will readily visit garden feeders to gorge on the food that has been put out for other birds.

The other two woodpeckers that you might encounter are the Green Woodpecker and the Lesser Spotted Woodpecker. The Green Woodpecker is a common resident, easily identified by its rather large size and mainly greenish plumage, whereas the Lesser Spot is like a sparrow-sized version of the Great Spot (and sadly now a rarity in the UK, mostly confined to southern England).

Ring-necked Parakeet

Love them or hate them, these long-tailed, green parrots are now very much a part of urban life in the south-east, and London in particular. There are not too many places within the capital that you can now visit without hearing the screeching of birds passing overhead. They tend to roost communally in large numbers and are very regular visitors to gardens.

Tawny Owl

Of all the urban birds mentioned in this section, the Tawny Owl is perhaps the one that you are least likely to see – mainly due to its nocturnal habits and the fact that it roosts in dense cover during the day. However, it is a fairly common bird, even in towns and cities, and most of us are probably never very far away from a breeding pair. If you stand outside during the late winter and early spring, particularly where there are large trees you have a good chance of hearing a pair duetting, the female calling *"kew-wick"* and the male *"ho-hoo-hoo-hooo."*

Swift

Swifts are true masters of the air and real harbingers of summer, arriving as they do in the UK in late April having spent the previous six months or so whirling over a variety of African vistas. Just as suddenly as they appear, they all but disappear again by mid-August, heading back south. Swifts are all-dark birds that have a very distinctive stiff-winged flight action and piercing,

screeching calls that can often be heard as they hurtle at great speed over the rooftops.

Although great fliers, a Swift's legs and feet are very weak and not capable of supporting its body weight. If one does have the misfortune of landing on the ground it is in severe trouble. If you should come across a marooned bird, gently pick it up and, with the wind behind you, softly toss it into the air. With any luck it will take to the skies with relative ease.

Swifts usually only land when visiting their nesting sites, typically located in crevices under the eaves of houses or within church towers. Their feet are designed for clinging onto vertical rather than flat surfaces, and brick or stone walls are ideal. Unfortunately, it is becoming increasingly hard for these birds to find access to suitable places to breed, with many nooks and crannies in buildings having been blocked up. As a result, the numbers of this enigmatic migrant have fallen dramatically in recent years. But all is not lost, as it is possible to encourage Swifts to breed by installing nestboxes, as explained later in this book.

House Martin

Famous for the mud nests that they build under the eaves of buildings, House Martins were once a common summer visitor along many a suburban street. Sadly, that is now largely a thing of the past, as they have decreased in many areas at an alarming rate. The reason is not entirely clear but could be due to changes in the design of, and materials used in, our modern housing, and the lack of available mud in our sanitized world. But there are still small breeding colonies in parts of most towns and cities, so look out for these delightful birds swooping over the rooftops between mid-April and October. As with the Swift, nestboxes can be provided to encourage them to breed.

House Martins are often confused with Swallows but have a white rump and throat (come to think of it, they bear more than a passing resemblance to a tiny flying Orca!).

Swallow

With their forked tails and swooping, dashing flight, Swallows are often confused for Swifts and vice versa by the unwary. They can, though, be told apart quite easy as the Swallow has a white breast. Both are summer visitors, with the Swallow arriving a little earlier than the Swift and staying well into October. Swallows can also be mistaken for House Martins, but don't have an obvious white rump.

This is a familiar bird for many living in the country, and in fact its international name is the Barn Swallow. However, although many pass through our urban landscape en route to their rural breeding grounds, some do actually stay to nest in our towns and cities, although usually on the outskirts.

Great Tit

The Great Tit, along with the Blue Tit, is among the most common birds to be seen in urban gardens. As its name suggest, the Great Tit is the larger of the two species, approaching a sparrow in size. It is instantly recognized by its yellow belly split by a black line, which extends beyond the legs as a black 'blob' in the male but just fizzles out in the female.

Great Tits nest in holes and can often be encouraged to breed by erecting nestboxes in suitable places in gardens or woodland.

Blue Tit

If Blue Tits were rare birds people would travel miles to catch sight of one. They are truly avian gems and a pleasure to watch cavorting at the feeders. Being mostly yellow and blue with white cheeks and the facial area framed in black, these little birds are quite easy to recognize.

Blue Tits, like all 'true' tits, are hole nesters and are often the first to investigate and stake a claim to nestboxes sited on a tree or the wall of a house.

Long-tailed Tit

There cannot be a cuter British urban bird than the Long-tailed Tit: a veritable small bundle of feathers with a spiky tail sticking out the back. Long-tailed Tits are social birds, travelling in troops and following each other one by one from bush to bush. Outside the breeding season other small woodland birds often join these flocks when they are foraging among the foliage in search of food.

Long-tailed Tits, despite their name, are not closely related to the Blue and Great Tits with which they often associate. They build very different intricate nests that are positioned deep within bushes or brambles. The exquisite structure is oval with a hole near the top and is fairly 'elastic', being constructed using spiders' webs, lichens, feathers and moss.

Robin

This cheeky chappie needs no introduction and is a bird that most people can recognise instantly. I say most people, but a few years ago I had to suffer acute embarrassment when my mum described a 'mystery' bird in her garden. She said it came up to her when she was digging up the weeds and had a red breast!

Robins are much studied and fascinating birds. Both sexes sing (the females warble when they hold territory) and they are renowned for being particularly pugnacious when in defence of their territory.

In a recent vote by the public to choose Britain's National Bird, the Robin topped the poll!

Song Thrush

Popularly just called the 'Thrush', this bird is another avian urbanite that is vaguely familiar to a lot of people – its spotted chest being the big giveaway. The main confusion comes when you meet a Mistle Thrush. It, too, has a spotted chest but is a larger bird with greyer upperparts (the Song Thrush is brown above), and is usually far less numerous.

Song Thrushes have a pleasant song that is fairly easy to recognize as individual notes and phrases are repeated two or three times over.

Blackbird

A very common bird that has one of the most melodious and fluty songs in Britain. The males are black with a yellow bill and the females brown with a duller bill. Fairly obvious in our gardens and parks, Blackbirds are actually thrushes and, like the Song Thrush, were originally woodland birds before the rise of urbanity.

Wheatear

I have thrown in this migratory, open country bird as they frequently pass through our towns and cities en route to and from their wilderness nesting sites. A truly gorgeous little wanderer, these birds fly phenomenal distances from Africa to Northern Europe, and back, each year. Some individuals travel to breed as far north as Greenland, racking up an 18,000-mile round trip – making them one of the farthest-travelling small migrant birds in the world.

The males in breeding plumage are particularly handsome, with their blue-grey upperparts and black wings and 'bandit' mask, whilst the females are duller. Watch out for them during the spring and autumn as they busily run around on sports fields, regularly pausing and standing bolt upright. Get too close and they will fly off, revealing their white rump and an inverted black 'T' on an otherwise white tail.

Pied Wagtail

Almost like a sparrow-sized Magpie, these birds are a familiar sight at virtually any supermarket car park or within the grounds of trading estates. They also love foraging on playing fields, snapping after insects and wagging that long, white-fringed, black tail like a bouncy toy. During the winter, Pied Wagtails often congregate in large night-time roosts in trees in inner city areas to take advantage of the warmth generated by nearby buildings.

Goldcrest

This mite of the bird world is the smallest bird in Britain, measuring just 9 cm and weighing only 6 grammes. They love to feed in the canopy of trees and can be quite difficult to track down as they flit from branch to branch uttering their high-pitched calls. After the breeding season they often band together with roving tit flocks and are then generally easier to see.

Look for a tiny ball of greenish feathers and, if you get a really good look, you might be lucky enough to spot the narrow crest that gives the bird its name – which is orangey-red on a male and yellow on a female.

Blackcap

This little bird has a gorgeous warbling song and in days of old was referred to as the Northern Nightingale – and for good reason, methinks. It is slightly smaller and slimmer than a sparrow but mostly grey, with the males sporting a black cap and the females a brown one.

Although mainly a summer visitor that winters in Africa, an increasing number migrate to Britain, apparently from mainland Europe, to spend the winter feeding at our bird tables. So don't be surprised if you see one in your garden, even on a frosty day.

Wren

The Wren is the most common bird in Britain, with upwards of 8 million territories. Although tiny, it is not, as many people think, our smallest breeding bird – a mantle that goes to the Goldcrest at 9 cm. The second smallest bird is not the Wren either, but the Goldcrest's cousin, the Firecrest. No, measuring up at just 10 cm, the wren is the third smallest bird in the land!

Although Wrens are not particularly shy, they are often overlooked as they forage furtively around the garden fence or in dense cover. They do, however, have an extremely loud song for such a small bird, which is very distinctive and a good one to learn.

Dunnock

Also known as the Hedge Sparrow, this is a bird that can often be spotted creeping around on the ground below the bird table. As the name suggests, at first glance it looks rather dull and nondescript – but take a closer look and you will see browns and greys. If seen well, the Dunnock actually has a very subtle beauty. Note also the thin, dark insectivorous bill, very different from the conical bill of a House Sparrow, which is a seedeater.

Jay

Many people are surprised to learn that these birds are actually now quite urbanized. There are also a lot of raised eyebrows when it is revealed that they are members of the crow family, albeit a gaudily plumaged one – with their pinkish-grey plumage and electric blue flash in the wings. Jays are typically woodland birds, and those in towns and cities still have that secretive woodland gene within their psyche – and hence have retained the ability to keep well hidden, and are often difficult to see well.

Magpie

One for sorrow, two for joy…. The Magpie is a bird tainted by myth and folklore, most of which is unfortunately fairly negative and pretty unfair. This bird, along with the Sparrowhawk, has been blamed for the general demise of our songbirds and, singularly, are labelled as sneaky thieves. But take another look at them. Firstly, they have a stunning piebald plumage that shimmers iridescent blue and green in the sunlight. Secondly, they are highly intelligent and fascinating birds to watch. OK, they are opportunistic predators, but they take the weak and unwary, thereby keeping the general health of our urban birds at a high standard. I think we should salute the Magpie.

Jackdaw

This is Britain's smallest crow. It is about the size of a Feral Pigeon and has a distinctive grey wash to the back of its neck and blue eyes. It is not usually an inner city bird but is often a frequent sight in the suburbs and smaller towns and villages.

Carrion Crow

Patrolling the skies, streets and playing fields, this is the typical large 'crow' that you are likely to see in most towns and cities across the land. They can be confused with Rooks, which are also large and black, but, unlike elsewhere in Europe, in the UK Rooks are generally farmland birds that are not too happy in the presence of people. They also differ from Carrion Crows in having an area of pasty white bare skin on their face.

You may sometimes come across crows with patches of white feathering on their wings and/or body. This is not a new species of urban crow, but poor diet affecting the pigmentation in their plumage.

Starling

Everybody loves Starlings and their popularity has grown with the public's recent fascination with the vast flocks – or murmurations – that congregate at some of their traditional roosting sites. It is awe-inspiring to watch these flocks constantly cutting shapes in the sky until a silent command sees them all suddenly shoot down into the roost – almost as though they had been sucked there by an invisible and irresistible tractor beam.

Starlings are also hard to resist when you see them in bright sunlight, the oily looking black plumage exuding a wonderful purple-green iridescence. Once you get to know your local Starlings you may notice that males have an eye-catching yellow bill with a blue base and that females are slightly less bright with a brownish base to the bill. You will also find that in winter both sexes look drabber and have flecks of white in their plumage.

House Sparrow

This is the universal LBJ or 'little brown job' – well at least the females are. The male's black bib, grey crown and russet brown wings make it quite a distinctive bird. Sparrows were once so common that no one even gave them a second glance, but unfortunately things are very different these days as they have declined alarmingly in most parts of the UK. So spare them the time of day when you next come across a boisterous flock.

Chaffinch

The male is a very pretty finch with its pink and brown hues. As with most songbirds, the female's browner plumage is a poor attempt when it comes to use of the colour palate, but they do still have prominent white wing flashes which makes them quite easy to recognize. Chaffinches can be quite approachable in town and city parks where they have become used to accepting handouts from gleeful park users.

Goldfinch

This colourful little finch is thankfully still a common sight in many urban gardens, as well as adjacent areas where seeding weeds are prevalent. With their red face and yellow wing markings they are quite easy to identify. They also have a distinctive call and even when walking down a busy high street you may hear their telltale tinkling notes above the city's din.

Greenfinch

In many of our large towns and cities the Greenfinch is often the only small bird to be seen flying overhead or sitting on rooftops or in tall trees. Although still a common garden bird, numbers have declined considerably in recent years due to an outbreak of the disease Trichomoniasis, which is caused by a parasite. As its name suggests, a Greenfinch is essentially green – well, at least the male is; females being duller and more brownish. Both sexes have a yellow flash along the edge of their wings.

Watch out for the male's springtime display flight when he launches himself from the top of a bush or tree to fly in a loop with a curious stiff-winged, bat-like wing action, twittering the whole time.

URBAN GARDEN BIRDING

I have always had a great love affair with gardens as my first proper patch was the one at the back of my mum's house in Wembley, north-west London. As a five-year-old I discovered quite by accident that my house doubled as a perfect gigantic heated hide and a café with an endless supply of tea. I used to spend hours at my bedroom window watching with my massive pair of binoculars over the range of back gardens, of which mine was a composite part. As I was too short, I had to stand on the central heating pipes to be able to gaze through the window. My garden was long and narrow, bordered on both sides with hedges that separated us from the neighbours. My mum had planted a rhododendron, a shrub that is not at all great for wildlife, and there was a large cooking apple tree quite close to the house. Towards the far end of the garden was a second shed (the first was near the back door of the house) and a reasonably sized vegetable patch that I periodically and begrudgingly had to water.

The portion of the garden immediately outside the back door had a small lawn and also sported a couple of kept flowerbeds that were great for insects, including lots of butterflies. Crucially, mum allowed me to claim a small patch that I cultivated to encourage weeds and native wild flowers to grow, having read about creating such areas in my Young Ornithologists' Club membership magazines. This patch was a hotbed for insects and other invertebrates, all good fodder for garden birds. I discovered my first froghoppers here after thinking that the frothy substance the plants were covered in was actually spit from a

I wish my garden had looked like this!

Cuckoo. So, I would balance there at my bedroom window, watching and waiting for birds to arrive. I quickly learnt that the best times to observe birds was invariably in the morning when nobody was out mowing the lawn or pruning their rose bushes.

I saved up cash, hard-earned from my paperboy job, to buy bird seed and cheap plastic nut bags from the local corner shop. The nut bags that I bought were the type that would probably be banned today for being dangerous to birds. Thinking about it now, the plastic mesh was so thick and serrated it was a wonder that it did not take some poor bird's foot off! I would hang these bags on my apple tree and watch as they became covered in Greenfinches, sparrows and tits. I also hung a dubiously constructed home-made bird table from a branch of the tree and was rewarded with comical views of Blackbirds balancing precariously on my unstable feeding station. My garden birds instantly became easier to see: House Sparrows, Blue and Great Tits and Greenfinches were practically resident, as were Wood Pigeons, Robins, Starlings, Blackbirds and Dunnocks. I also noticed a number of birds flying over my house, including lots of Starlings and Feral Pigeons. There were some drawbacks to my early morning pre-school birding with outsized binoculars strapped around my neck. I had to be careful where I pointed them for fear of being noticed by the neighbours living opposite and being wrongly exposed as a peeping Tom. The moral of this story is always spare a thought as to where you aim your binoculars in residential areas!

Gardens are great places to cut your teeth studying and identifying the more common avian inhabitants of your local neighbourhood. Making your garden into a haven for birds is quite easy, although it will take more than just putting up a bag of nuts every now and again when the weather turns bad. With a little commitment on your part in the shape of planting appropriate flora, regularly putting out food, supplying fresh water and providing nesting sites you could soon be hosting a variety of birds in your garden. In the past, the perceived wisdom was that you should only feed birds during the winter months. But most experts now agree that it is OK to feed the birds throughout the year, the thinking being that they will come and feed when they need to. If plenty of natural food is available then that will be the bird's first choice.

It is worth pointing out at this stage that not all gardens are equal when it comes to attracting birds. If you live in an area with other habitats nearby, such as a wood or patch of scrub, and the gardens that surround you are managed with wildlife in mind, then the chances are that you will also reap the avian rewards. If you are the only kid on the block with a wildlife garden you may attract more birds than anyone else, but the range of species may not be particularly diverse. Different species will be found in your garden depending on the time of year and where you are situated within the UK. The vast majority of gardens in Britain will not have visitations by Crested Tits, for instance – an unusual-looking member of the tit family replete with a stripy crest. The reason for this is that in the UK this bird is only found in Scottish Caledonian Forest that lies mostly within the Cairngorms National Park. However, if your garden were in Paris or on the outskirts of Amsterdam then Crested Tits could well be on the visual menu. Why? Because it is much more common elsewhere within its extensive European range, and in Paris can even be found in city centre parks.

Conversely, if you want to find a Robin within a European garden then there is no better place than in a British one. Our Robins are often confiding birds that provide hours of pleasure by allowing a close approach, often accepting the morsels that we offer them – but in Europe it is much more of a woodland bird and considerably shyer. Do not be fooled by the Robin's charm, though. When one sits on your spade handle looking at you sweetly while you dig up the weeds, it is not giving you love. Far from it, as you are, quite literally, being treated like a pig! Like the continental Robins, our birds were originally woodland birds and habitually followed Wild Boar and deer, feeding on the worms and other invertebrates that the mammals dug up or disturbed. Similar easy pickings can be had from a nation of gardeners.

The Robin, Britain's national bird (as voted back in 2015) and its favourite garden bird and Christmas card pin-up, has long been known for its aggressive territorial behaviour towards not only its own kind but against other garden birds as well. Robins hold territories throughout the year, and even the females sing and fend off interlopers invading their space. And it is during the winter, especially around Christmas, when they begin to pair up. Yes, if there is one bird that you would chose as the quintessential British garden bird it would be the Robin. I have been regaled many times by proud garden birders telling me about the same Robin that has been faithfully coming to their garden for years on end. Well, I'm afraid it's time to dispel yet another urban myth. According to information collected by the British Trust for Ornithology, that faithful Robin hanging around your back door for many years was, in fact, probably many different individual birds. The average life span of a Robin is around two years, with the oldest individual known being just over eight years old. Add to the mix the fact that some of our British birds head south to Iberia for the winter, to be replaced by the shyer, greyer continental race, and there could potentially be quite a few Robins passing through our gardens.

Robin

Great Tits, along with their smaller Blue Tit cousins, are also, it seems, found in almost every garden. However, the Great Tit's breeding success has been shown to be lower in urban gardens than in their original woodland habitats. These birds depend upon the abundance of caterpillars that feed on the leaves of woodland trees in spring, just at the time when they are rearing their young. However, in urban areas there are many more non-native trees, and these don't support the same range of insects as native species. This means fewer caterpillars and less food, which has the knock-on effect of fewer chicks fledging. Conversely, the survival rate of tits is higher in urban gardens during the winter due to the supplementary food that we provide. This food source is such an attraction that it even draws birds out of the woods. The Great Tits that visit the bird feeders in our gardens undoubtedly stand a better chance of survival compared with those elsewhere.

Depending on where you live, one of the classic garden birds will be the House Sparrow. However, although once abundant throughout the UK, this familiar small brown bird has suffered a phenomenal decrease over the last 25 years, to the point that it has become very rare or is even extinct in certain parts of the country. It is thought that the lack of breeding sites, coupled with the diminishing number of insects on which they feed their young, could be the main reasons behind their demise. Fortunately, this situation is not mirrored across mainland Europe, since the House Sparrow is still fairly numerous in some cities.

The RSPB's Big Garden Birdwatch is an annual event that's been running since 1979, in which participants across the nation spend an hour over a weekend in late January counting both the number of species and individual birds that are present in their gardens.

Blackbird (male) sunbathing

Wood Pigeon with nesting material

Great Tit

133

Upwards of 500,000 people participate each year, and more than nine million birds are counted. Although not exhaustive, the survey gives a very good indication of the health of the population of our garden birds. Although House Sparrow, Starling and Blackbird have been among the top five most numerous species recorded during the Big Garden Birdwatch over the last few years, the information collected through the event has proved to be far more enlightening. It has shown, for example, that the numbers of some species, such as the House Sparrow, have been declining steadily year-on-year, whereas others have gradually increased; and it has also been used to highlight differences across the country. So, if you want to play your part, earmark an hour over the last weekend in January and start counting!

Birds are largely creatures of habit and outside the breeding season tend to have daily circuits that they follow routinely. Such behaviour is found in birds the world over, and often involves several species banding together, foraging as they move. If you are ever fortunate enough to find yourself in a tropical forest you may hear the local birders using the term 'bird waves'. Imagine you are walking through lush forest with dense undergrowth but don't see any movements or even hear a peep. Then, all of a sudden, a multi-species wave of birds moves through the foliage, all heading in the same direction. You may get a few stragglers at the end of the flock, and then they are gone, leaving the forest silent once again.

Even if a bird is a rarity, thousands of miles from home, they often develop a routine that sees them regularly visit certain places, such as a favoured bush or stretch of field, that they have discovered to be a good place to feed. That is why twitchers (rarity hunters) often stand for hours at the spot where their quarry was last seen, in the hope that the bird will return. This circuit-following behaviour can also be noticed in your garden. The main participants are usually Long-tailed Tits, along with Blue and Great Tits, but with them can be other species like Coal Tits, Nuthatches and Chiffchaffs and if you are really lucky, a Lesser Spotted Woodpecker.

You may quickly come to realize that your feeders are used at different times of day by different species. Some arrive first thing in the morning, whilst others come later in the day. Generally speaking, smaller birds store less fat than large birds, usually just enough to see them through one night, and have a higher metabolic rate. On a really cold night a bird can lose up to 5% of its body fat and many need to consume as much as 30% of its body weight

Long-tailed Tit

in food every day just to survive. So, come the dawn, they need to feed immediately to make up for the shortfall. In the case of the Blue Tit, individuals have to spend up to 85% of the daylight hours looking for food. Larger birds can afford to arrive later because they have the ability to store more fat. However, all these patterns can be thrown into flux by adverse weather, and particularly low overnight temperatures, the presence of predators and the conditions at roosting sites. It is the cold that is the killer – if a bird cannot find enough food to replenish its lost energy store then it will be facing the final curtain.

Small birds have a couple of adaptations that help them to combat the cold in our northern latitudes. Their main defence is the insulation provided by their feathers: by fluffing up their plumage they trap a layer of air that helps to prevent heat loss. This is the equivalent of us donning a puffer jacket to keep warm. Smaller species also have an undercoat of downy feathers that becomes denser during the winter months. I was fascinated to learn that the weight of a House Sparrow's plumage increases by 70% following the autumn moult, setting it up to keep warm during the winter. So think again the next time you see a fat Robin sitting on a branch in the snow.

Most species of bird show three peaks of feeding activity during a typical winter's day. The initial peak occurs first thing in the morning with the smaller birds replenishing their lost energy reserves. The second peak is a shorter one during the middle of the day, which is a more dangerous time to be out and about due to the increased risk of predation. Finally, there is a peak the end of the day when the birds load up on their energy reserves before the long night ahead. By having a feeding station that is always stocked with food and water, the cyclical visitations by garden birds will be more predictable than if you were trying to see the same species foraging for natural food sources. The situation becomes less predicable during the spring and summer when many garden birds are raising broods. The parent birds are now active practically from dawn until dusk, largely looking elsewhere for insects and other invertebrates to feed their young. This is the reason that activity at your feeders slackens off, although adults will still visit occasionally to find food for themselves.

During the course of a year you may notice that the populations of your urban garden birds change, with some species only being present in a particular season. For instance, in the winter visitors from northern Europe, such as Redwings, Fieldfares and Bramblings

House Sparrow (male)

Blue Tit

Robin

(a close relative of our more familiar Chaffinch), will be rubbing shoulders (or more correctly, wings) with your resident birds. As my good friend Bill Oddie once commented, if birds spoke in human language your garden would be filled with accents from across the continent. The biggest surprise to many people, though, would be that some of the individuals of species that you generally think of as residents, such as Robins and Blackbirds, would also be sporting foreign accents. In fact, the only truly consistent British voices would probably belong to Wood Pigeons and House Sparrows, birds that rarely move far from their natal areas.

Spring and autumn will also bring a fresh influx of visitors, some of which are clearly just passing through. My current garden is situated in urban west London, and is effectively a concrete square patio surrounded by the backs of houses and the outer walls of the neighbour's gardens – so I'm pretty much boxed in. There is not much in the way of vegetation in any of the gardens in my block, with most people opting for ornamental pot plants, although there is a high incidence of trellises adorning peoples' garden walls, flowing with voluminous ivy. When I first moved in, however, there was a medium-sized tree in an adjacent garden that provided me with regular sightings of Great Spotted Woodpecker, but sadly it was cut down for reasons unknown. But, even in the middle of this urbanity, I notice seasonal changes in the species I record. When kicking a football around in the garden with my mate during the spring and autumn I occasionally see migrating Swallows, House Martins and Sand Martins, birds that don't breed anywhere in the neighbourhood. On rare occasions a weird migrant has shown up, looking completely out of sorts as it briefly inspected the concrete for morsels. A good example is a female Black Redstart that I watched foraging in a neighbour's guttering one autumn. This just goes to show that migrants can – and do – turn up in the most unlikely of places.

Watching your garden regularly will almost certainly bring the odd surprise to brighten your day. What started as rare reports from homeowners of Blackcaps feeding at bird tables during the winter is now recognized as a normal occurrence, and reflects a sea-change shift

Blackcap (male)

Black Redstart (female)

Fieldfare

Bullfinch (male)

in the migration habits of a warbler that used to be considered just a summer visitor. Although our summer-visiting Blackcaps still head south for the winter to sub-Saharan Africa, some birds from Eastern Europe are now heading west instead of south and ending up in the UK. Even more remarkable is the fact that these birds are developing thicker, stronger bills to deal with the non-insectivorous food that we put out in our bird feeders. Interestingly, the number of winter records for this warbler in urban and suburban gardens was higher than from those in rural areas. This reflects the abundance of food to be found at the feeding stations in towns and cities, coupled with the urban heat island effect.

Many people are concerned when Blackbirds seemingly disappear from their garden during late summer. However, I am pleased to say that this is not because there has been a sudden population crash. Like many of our songbirds, by this time in the season a Blackbird's plumage has become worn and scruffy after a frenetic period of raising its broods. So, in order to be in good enough condition to make it through the coming winter, it moults its feathers. When its wing feathers in particular are being replaced, a bird is very prone to predation, and as a precaution it tends to keep out of sight in deep cover. Once autumn arrives and the moult is complete, many urban birds then move out into the countryside to plunder berries, often forming flocks with other Blackbirds. It is only with the onset of the first frosts that these birds begin to return to our gardens, but by this time they are often accompanied by winter-visiting Blackbirds of Scandinavian, central European or even Russian origin.

By late summer and early autumn, sparrows and finches, too, will often move from suburban gardens to nearby farmland, but in this case searching for grain before it is harvested. Sparrows and finches from the heart of urban areas will also move around, but generally fairly short distances to areas where weed seeds are available. You are therefore more likely to find flocks feeding on rough ground and brownfield sites rather than in your garden. Tits also seemingly become scarce later in the summer and during early autumn, as once the breeding season is over they move to forage high in the canopies of trees – you will need to look up if you want to find them!

Autumn is usually the time of plenty in the bird world. If the weather remains mild and their natural food supply is good, birds will not need to visit your feeders. It therefore makes sense only to put out a little food at this time of year, and not to fill feeders to the brim. At the very least, you will not feel so bad if your offerings are left untouched. As I explained earlier, birds do tend to follow regular feeding circuits, and if they notice that you have food in your garden they will soon return when the going begins to get tough – you just need to make sure that you keep it fresh by changing it from time to time.

Attracting birds to your garden

Providing food and water

Feeding birds has come a long way since the days of simply chucking kitchen scraps out of the back door. It is now something of a national pastime, and a multi-million pound industry. Pappy white bread is thankfully no longer the mainstay of bird table cuisine, as it is a really appalling food source. The bird foods that we have available today are far more nutritious, and by offering a wide range we can provide a healthy diet for many of our much-loved birds. Even where the food you provide is just a supplement to a bird's natural diet, it can make a huge difference to its chances of survival, particularly during the cold, dark winter days, or to maintaining its condition during the breeding season when there are so many hungry youngsters to feed.

It is important to consider the range of bird species that may visit your garden when planning the menu you offer, as each has particular requirements and feeds in slightly different ways. Broadly speaking, birds with conical bills, such as sparrows and finches, are essentially seed and nut eaters, whereas birds with slender bills, like Robins, thrushes and Dunnocks, are usually insectivorous and will make a beeline for the mealworms first. There is some crossover, though, as most seedeaters will take insect prey during the breeding season. House Sparrow chicks, for example, need insect or other invertebrate food when they are developing, as this provides vital protein that helps them survive their first year of life. Indeed, studies have shown that in gardens where mealworms are provided, a higher number of chicks fledge successfully.

The contraptions that you use to provide food will also have a bearing on the types of bird that come to your garden. Some species, such as tits and finches, cling to or perch on feeders and dangling fat-balls to peck at seeds and nuts, whilst Robins and thrushes prefer to visit tables or trays for invertebrate food, such as mealworms. Wood Pigeons and Dunnocks, as well as Robins and thrushes, like to forage on the ground for spilt seed and any mealworms that might have fallen from the table.

Seeds tend to attract a wider range of birds than just peanuts on their own, and many urban garden birders provide black sunflower seeds or sunflower hearts as the main course. Quality peanuts, niger seeds and high-energy seed mixes are also equally valuable. I have found that sultanas are irresistible to ground-feeders like Song Thrushes and Blackbirds, but be careful because they can be toxic to dogs. The provision of some grated cheese (although avoiding anything salted) will hopefully be welcomed by Robins – as I demonstrated successfully on BBC1's The One Show a few years ago, when I attracted one into a south London garden with grated Edam. Windfall apples are always an attraction to thrushes and

Goldfinch

Starling

Song Thrush

Peanuts

Sunflower hearts

Starlings, especially during harsh weather. The types bird food that you could consider providing are summarized here.

Peanuts are a mainstay at the feeding station, and high in the oils and proteins needed by birds. Make sure that you get good quality peanuts from a reputable source. Peanuts are best offered in a fine mesh feeder that only allows the birds to take pieces away and never a whole nut, but can also be supplied as granules or peanut cake.

Black sunflower seed revolutionized bird feeding when it was introduced to the mass market in the early 1990s, and is absolutely adored by Greenfinches and tits. It provides a high-energy food in a readily accessible form and can be purchased as part of a seed mix or on its own.

Sunflower hearts are derived from black sunflower seeds and are more expensive. They do, however, have two advantages over the seeds themselves: firstly, and most importantly, since there is no husk to peel away, birds can feed more quickly; and secondly, there is no pile of husks under the feeder for us to clear up.

Dunnock feeding on black sunflower seeds

142

Niger seed

Seed and grain mix

Mealworms

Niger seed is a newbie in the bird food world. It is rich in oil and ideal for birds with delicate bills – and is particularly loved by Goldfinches. In view of the seed's small size it has to be offered in specially designed feeders to stop it from falling through the holes. You can provide this seed as part of a mix or sprinkle it on the ground for Dunnocks.

Seed and grain mixes are a variable feast and available in a wide range of combinations, with some being better than others. The cheaper mixes tend to have a high element of cereal content which is likely to attract hordes of pigeons. Better quality mixes that contain less cereal are much more attractive to finches, tits and buntings.

Mealworms are gourmet food to many birds. They are craved by a wide range of other insectivorous birds – supply them and your Robins will love you forever!

Fresh coconut can be provided by chopping one up or sawing it in half and hanging it upside down. Then you just need to sit back and wait for a troop of Long-tailed Tits to discover it.

Great Tit and Blue Tit feeding on coconut

143

There are a few types of food that should be avoided in order to keep your birds looking in great shape. The definite no-nos include cooked oats, which can dry and solidify around a bird's bill, sugary treats, loose whole peanuts (as these can potentially choke chicks), white bread and any salty foods such as salted peanuts and bacon rind. Desiccated coconut should also be avoided (since it can swell up inside the bird and cause dehydration), as should any mouldy foods (as these can harbour harmful bacteria).

Feeders

There are a variety of ways to present food to your garden birds. The most basic is to set up a platform feeder (bird table), be it on a post or suspended from a sturdy branch. The main advantage of this kind of feeder is that you can get a clear view of all the visitors, but there are some drawbacks. As everything is thrown onto the same surface the food can quickly become a mush when it rains. As a consequence, the table will need to be cleaned more often and food replenished more frequently. Also, a table is more likely than other types of feeder to be dominated by pigeons, Magpies, Grey Squirrels and, if you live in the south, Ring-necked Parakeets.

A variation on the platform feeder theme, hopper feeders have a container that stores and trickle-feeds the food, and a roof that protects it from the elements. Although this type of feeder requires less cleaning than bird tables, you may not always be able to see the birds on the side of the feeder that faces away from your house. There are many types and sizes of tube feeders available and they are a magnet for tits and finches, attracted to the nuts or seeds they contain. Although tube feeders are usually free-hanging, some are available that can be secured to windows.

Platform feeder with Nuthatch and Blue and Great Tits

The location of your feeding station is important. It is a good idea to try and rotate its position around the garden over time or, if possible, to have several feeding points in order to avoid the build-up of droppings in any one area. Feeders should be at least 1·5m (4' 6") above the ground to be out of leaping reach of most cats, but at a height that makes it easy for you to replenish stocks. Ideally, they should also be at least 3m (10 feet) away from the nearest overhanging tree branch or other solid structure to thwart the intentions of any enterprising squirrel.

Try to avoid putting out food for ground-feeding birds in the evening, as your intended diners may have already slipped off to roost and instead you will be providing a banquet for a motley crew of local rats. It is also best to avoid sprinkling food liberally on the ground, placing it instead in a container, such as a dish or a small upturned dustbin lid. By treating it as a 'ground bird table' you can more easily remove the food in the evenings, thereby avoiding a potential rat problem. Incidentally, the notion that you are never farther away than six feet from a rat is a fallacy. It has been calculated that the actual distance is more like 160 feet – but even that is still too close for most people!

Most importantly, don't forget that an empty feeding station doesn't attract birds!

Grey Squirrel

Birdbaths

Water is the liquid of life and something that all living things need to survive. Every garden should have water on offer year-round, at it can be provided in a number of ways, ranging from flamboyant ornate birdbaths to an old baking tray, and everything in between.

Although birdbaths come in countless shapes and sizes, and are an important source of drinking water, they are, as their name suggests, equally important as places for birds to bathe – which is essential if they are to keep their plumage in tip-top condition. The ideal birdbath has a sloping base that results in a variety of water depths ranging from 2·5 cm (1 inch) to 10 cm (4 inches), since this provides suitable bathing conditions for birds of different sizes. Adding a couple of stones to vary the topography and provide convenient perches is also a good idea. As birds are particularly vulnerable to predation when bathing, your birdbath should be placed in a prominent position so that both you and the birds can look out for any possible enemies. It should also be located so that it can be easily replenished and cleaned (both of which should be done on a regular basis).

House Sparrow (male) bathing

145

Nestboxes

Our gardens and buildings have been shown to be very important places for breeding birds nationally. Most of our House Martin and Swift populations now inhabit our towns and cities, and a significant proportion of our breeding Starlings and House Sparrows nest in urban areas. And birds such as Blackbirds and Peregrines nest in higher densities in our urban areas than they do in the open countryside. There is obviously something about city living that is helping these species to colonize our urban surroundings successfully. But, that said, we still need to give them all the help we can.

No urban wildlife garden can be complete without offering its visitors the opportunity to nest and rest. Although some species will find ideal spots to do so if your garden has plentiful vegetation, the placing of nestboxes can help no end to make your garden even more appealing to birds. The main problem for many species is that Britain is suffering from a chronic shortage of holes! Local authorities, keen on adhering to their public safety mandates, all too often remove old trees in parks and local woods that are deemed to be dangerous. However, these old trees, once they start to decay, are important for woodpeckers and other hole-nesting birds, as rotting wood is readily excavated and enables the birds to create nesting chambers. Coupled with this is the fact that most modern buildings are constructed without cavities in which birds like Starlings and House Sparrows can nest; Hopefully, you will begin to get the picture, and this is why it is so important for us to provide artificial nesting sites.

Broadly speaking, there are three types of nestbox: the classic 'tit' box with a small round hole in the front; the open-fronted box, which is reminiscent of a letterbox but with a much bigger slot, which are great for birds like Robins and if you're lucky Spotted Flycatcher; and the various specialist designs for species such as Swift and Tawny Owl. The size of the hole, along with the size of the box, determines the species that will use it. For birds like tits and sparrows, the box itself can be quite small, with a minimum floor dimension of

Nestbox and Great Tit

Nestbox with reinforced hole and Blue Tit

15 cm × 12 cm. The base of the box should be at least 12 cm below the bottom of the entrance hole so that predators such as cats cannot reach in to scoop out nestlings. For larger species like Starlings, the box needs to be proportionately bigger.

Ideally, nestboxes should be made of wood at least 15 mm thick, with the exterior treated with a coat of non-toxic, water-based wood preservative. It is important to avoid using paint, as this can be toxic, and not to treat the inside of the box. The box should have a slanting roof to allow rainwater to run off. If you are making one yourself have fun and don't worry if the end result is not an example of perfect carpentry – provided it is waterproof, it will do. The roof should essentially be a lid that can be lifted off in order to inspect the box to see if it is occupied or to clean it. Some birds, notably Robins, will readily nest in weird objects – upturned kettles and old boots spring to mind. A friend of mine even had a customized guitar without strings put up in her garden that attracted a pair of Robins. Steer clear of the fussily ornate birdhouses that are advertised in the back pages of the Sunday supplements. Some are utterly ridiculous, combining bird table with nestbox, which at best are invariably more a case of style over substance.

The best places to pick up a decent nestbox are either through a reputable purveyor of garden bird equipment or from your local garden or DIY centre. Look for well-made boxes the dimensions of which fit the requirements of the species that you are wishing to attract – and avoid those with a perch near the hole, as this will only serve to give predators easier access to any nestlings within. To minimize the risk of Great Spotted Woodpeckers or squirrels chiselling or gnawing at the hole to make it bigger, you can buy boxes with the holes rimmed with metal, or fix a metal plate with a hole to the front of the box yourself. Either option is a more than efficient way of repelling any hammering a woodpecker would choose to throw at it.

Many garden birders stress over the best place to site their nestbox. Although positioning the box so that it faces north-east is generally considered to be the ideal, in reality the direction makes little difference so long as it's not facing directly into the prevailing south-westerly wind.

Open-fronted nestbox and Spotted Flycatcher

House Martin feeding chick in artificial nestbox

It should, however, be sheltered from direct rain and direct sunlight, otherwise there's a risk that the chicks inside the box will cook. Consider the best use of available cover in a quiet spot so that it can be sited away from the prying eyes of potential predators, but make sure that there is still a clear flight path to the box. Also, ensure that the box is in a location that is easy for you to access for maintenance purposes. If you can, position your box so that you can sneakily enjoy the goings on from the comfort of your living room. Resist the temptation to put your box near a bird table or feeder since birds are territorial around their nest sites and will not take kindly to a continuous procession of other birds outside their nest hole. Under these circumstances they will spend too much time guarding their space and not enough time on family duties. Another point to note is to avoid putting up too many boxes up in the same area. Many species will not relish having neighbours literally inches from their front door, so take care when spreading the housing around!

There is a lot to be said for putting up nestboxes in the early spring – after all it is the time of love, with thoughts of starting little families filling the air. However, although you can install nestboxes at any time of the year, I feel that autumn is best. This is the time when birds are roaming their territories in search of food, and during their circuits not only do they come across the various feeding stations in their domain but also potential nest sites – including your nestboxes. This is especially the case with young birds that are exploring for the first time. In the winter, birds may use nestboxes for roosting, and this provides another opportunity for them to scope out possible nesting sites. Autumn is also a good time to take down your existing boxes for a maintenance check. Remove any old nests, dead chicks and egg fragments and rinse the box out with boiling water to kill off any parasites. Putting in a bed of dry straw may tempt birds to take up residence – think of this as though you were moving into a new house that already has furniture and a fitted kitchen. Every little helps to make the birds feel just that little bit cozier!

Nestbox in situ

As I have intimated earlier, several of our British garden birds are in sharp decline and you can help to reverse their fortunes. Whilst urban garden birders can help the House Sparrow directly by the provision of food, planting insect-attracting flora and installing nestboxes, for other species it is a little more complicated. Although species like Swifts and House Martins are not true garden birds as such, and you won't be able to provide them with food, you can tempt them to nest. Swift boxes are of a different size and shape to your average nestbox and are often constructed out of concrete. You can either mount the box – or better still boxes, as Swifts nest colonially – under your eaves or have them sunk into the brickwork of your house. These boxes are rectangular with either a hole or a slit in one corner near the underside so that the birds can swoop up and crawl inside.

The House Martin is a bird that I almost took for granted when, as a kid, I wandered my local streets in Wembley looking for clusters of their cupped mud-nests under the eaves of houses. But nowadays, I know of very few places in the Capital where they still breed. One of the reasons for their decline is believed to be a lack of available mud to construct their amazing nests. So bring on instead the artificial House Martin nest, which is now readily available and looks just like the real thing. The secret is not to place these nestboxes immediately above your front or back door, unless you like getting splattered – although sticking a shelf beneath should catch most of the droppings. As House Martins are colonial breeders, if you put up artificial nests you might even encourage other House Martins to build natural nests alongside.

If you want to take the provision of nestboxes to the next level then you could always get one with a camera and microphone installed so that you can link it to your TV or computer in order to enjoy hours of family fun – à la Springwatch. This will allow you to see and hear all the action, day and night, from the comfort of your home. Some of these boxes have detachable cameras that, when the breeding season is over, can be reattached

House Martin at nest

to specially designed bird tables, allowing you once again to watch all the action from your sofa. Provided your box is occupied, be prepared for some amazing footage that shows the life and death struggles that go on every day right under your nose.

Of course, not everyone has the luxury of owning a garden, as many of us live in housing blocks, apartments and estates where private gardens are in short supply. However, you can still help your local urban bird population by attaching a nestbox to the wall of the property in which you reside. Perhaps with the help of the local residents group or housing association you could also organize the placing of a selection of boxes in the communal gardens and community areas. Aside from the classic boxes discussed previously, you could support the local sparrow population by putting up a series of customized many-holed boxes – essentially terraced housing for House Sparrows. These are effectively three nestboxes bolted together, with the holes for the end chambers on the sides and the middle chamber having its hole in the usual place in the front. Put one of these constructions under the eaves of your house and, fingers crossed, you may soon have up to three pairs of grateful sparrows nesting. You could also instigate putting up Swift and House Martin boxes in the eaves of some of the buildings in your area, and by involving the local kids you are bound to attract an enthusiastic bunch of volunteers. This is a great way of encouraging youngsters to have a personal involvement in monitoring the progress of the birds nesting in their boxes.

Finally, don't be too disappointed if the birds fail to take advantage of your nestbox immediately. Sometimes you may have to wait a couple of seasons before anything pokes its head in or out. If you have no joy at all after two years, then it may be worth trying your luck elsewhere by re-siting the box. However, be patient with Swift boxes as they may stand empty for several years before being adopted. In some cities, such as Cambridge, specially designed Swift towers have been erected in order to encourage the establishment of new colonies of this dynamic urban bird. The towers are usually fitted with a sound system that belts out recordings of their screaming calls – a ploy to attract stray, unsettled pairs. This approach is needed as adult Swifts are very loyal to their nest sites and return to the same

Installing a nestbox for Grey Wagtails   Inside a nestbox used by Great Tits

little crevice in a church tower roof, crack in the gable of a house or, nowadays, nestbox year after year. However, when youngsters return from Africa for the first time, they effectively go property hunting. It is then that they may be attracted to the calls of other Swifts, spot your boxes and, if you're lucky, will set up home the following year.

Threats

Predators and nuisance species

Setting up a feeding station or providing nestboxes is a sure-fire way of attracting birds into your garden. But, having done so, many people then find they are attracting species they consider to be a problem. I'm often asked whether there are ways of dealing with problem species and short answer is not really. You can try putting chilli powder on your peanuts to dissuade Grey Squirrels: they hate the taste but birds are impervious to it. You could put up fortified 'squirrel proof' feeders, but although this may thwart them initially, squirrels are bright and cunning beasts and always seem to work out a way of cheating the system. This type of feeder may stop Ring-necked Parakeets and Feral and Wood Pigeons from accessing the food, but pigeons especially will simply glean the ground underneath for bits that other birds have chiselled off. Feeders should ideally be sited away from cover to reduce the problems caused by marauding squirrels and cats, but on the other hand your feathered friends will need a bush or two nearby in which they can hide to avoid ambush by a hunting Sparrowhawk – so it's often a difficult balance.

It is always very upsetting to come across dead or dying birds, but worse still to see one killed before your very eyes while it was happily feeding at the nut dispenser with its mates. Whether we like it or not,

Grey Squirrel raiding a squirrel-proof feeder!

Sparrowhawk (male)

151

predators such as Sparrowhawks have hunted small birds for aeons, Magpies, Jays and even Great Spotted Woodpeckers have raided nests since the devil was a boy, and the Grey Squirrel, a relatively new kid on the block, is also partial to the odd nestling. All these species have a place in your garden's ecology, and predation is part of the natural sequence of events. If you watch your garden for long enough you will occasionally see moribund chicks, sickly adult birds and predators taking down prey on your lawn. Resist the temptation to rush out, arms flailing, to shoo off that Sparrowhawk in an attempt to rescue its stricken quarry. The chances are that even if it does fly off the victim will still die due to the trauma it suffered or from the injuries it sustained. It was attacked for a reason: although appearing perfectly fine, it may have been ill or had some other impediment that was totally undetectable to our eyes.

So try to quell any murderous thoughts that you may develop towards predators such as the Sparrowhawk. Content yourself instead with the notion that they are killing only the weakest, oldest, least experienced or sickest birds. If every songbird survived, the population would soon become far too large for the supply of food available and the result would be mass starvation and disease. There is nothing you can do to exclude species like the Sparrowhawk, and nor should you try, as most sharp-witted birds on top physical form can get themselves out of harm's way in time. It is important to come to terms with seeing birds killed in your garden – is nature's way of maintaining thriving populations and, after all, Sparrowhawks are fantastic garden birds to watch too!

There are some people who actively blame the demise of our songbirds on Sparrowhawks and the corvids (crows, Magpie and Jay). However, scientific research has shown that there

Domestic Cat

152

is nothing to suggest that this is the case. The biggest impact on songbird numbers has come from the actions of man: destroying habitat, using pesticides and hunting. After us, Public Enemy Number One for garden birds has got to be the domestic moggie. A study undertaken by The Mammal Society estimated that the UK's cats catch up to 220 million prey items annually, of which around 65 million are birds. It is for this reason that many garden birders want to deter cats, particularly where the animals have worked that there are potentially easy pickings around feeding stations. However, a range of relatively simple measures can be implemented to reduce the risk of predation by cats.

Try to avoid putting food on the ground and situate your feeders away from fences or other structures from which a cat could leap – and of course away from possible ambush spots in order to give the birds a clear view of any incoming enemies. If your bird table is on a post, it is worth making the base as uncomfortable or as difficult for a cat to hang on to as possible – planting spiny shrubs like Holly is a good option for preventing loitering felines. A squirrel baffle, which is a Perspex cone placed midway up the post of a bird table, can stop both squirrels and cats from shimmying up. Planting thick, wildlife-friendly vegetation, such as prickly bushes and climbers around the perimeter of your garden, or at least in areas where cats could sneak in, is another good idea. As well as being a cat-proof barrier, the right shrubs can provide nest sites or food for the birds – whether this be insects or berries. If you own a cat the obvious thing to do is to keep it indoors, but if it does have to go out, put a bell on a collar around its neck to make it as noisy as possible and alert the birds to its presence.

Diseases

Garden birds can carry a variety of diseases that could be a threat to people or cats and dogs. These are caused by bacteria including *Salmonella*, *Campylobacter* and *Escherichia coli* (generally referred to as *E. coli*). It therefore makes sense to follow routine hygiene precautions when handling feeders and bird tables or feeding birds directly. Keeping your feeders clean will minimize the risk of any infection being transmitted, and also help to prevent the birds visiting your garden from passing diseases among themselves.

The following might sound like a military drill, or akin to scrubbing up to perform surgery, but adhering to these simple measures will enhance everybody's lives, not least those of the birds. Try to clean your feeders and feeding sites regularly by using a wildlife-friendly disinfectant, making sure that you rinse them thoroughly and

Diseased Greenfinch

153

allow them to air-dry before refilling. Wear rubber gloves when cleaning your feeders and wash your hands and forearms thoroughly with soap and water afterwards, and ideally again before eating and drinking. Make sure that any brushes and cleaning equipment you use for feeders, as well as bird baths, are not used for any other purpose, and store them outside the house well away from any your own food – ideally in a garden shed if you have one.

Although the provision of fresh water is an excellent way of attracting birds into your garden in order to drink and bathe, it is important to ensure that any containers used are kept as clean as possible. By emptying and drying your birdbath on a daily basis you will kill potentially harmful organisms, such as the parasitic protozoan *Trichomonas*. This single-celled animal causes the disease Trichomoniasis that affects birds, as well as humans. In the early 2000s there was a major epidemic across Britain and into Europe that affected many garden birds, with Greenfinches and Chaffinches being hardest hit. The victims show general signs of illness that include fluffed-up plumage and lethargy. Affected birds may drool saliva, have difficulty in swallowing or show laboured breathing. The disease may progress over several days or even weeks, with the affected individual often becoming very thin. The British population of Greenfinches was particularly badly affected and declined by 35% from 2006 to 2009, with the average number of the birds visiting our gardens falling by 50%. This massive drop in numbers represents the largest-scale mortality of British birds to infectious disease on record. It just goes to show how devastating a disease outbreak can be to our wildlife within a short time frame.

If you do get an outbreak of disease in your garden you should significantly reduce the amount of food that you put out, or ideally stop feeding altogether for two to four weeks. This will encourage the birds to disperse, and therefore minimize the chances of any new birds that arrive to use the feeding station becoming infected. Thereafter, gradually reintroduce feeding, but continue to monitor the general health of the birds that come to visit. Avoid handling any sick or injured birds without wearing rubber gloves or using an inverted plastic bag.

Cultivating wildlife-friendly gardens

The gardens that are most attractive to birds and other wildlife are those with a combination of bird feeders and wildlife-friendly vegetation. Sterile decking, boring lawns and ugly wooden fences are just not cool. Birds love the opportunity to forage in insect-rich foliage while waiting their turn to raid the bird table, so a combination of the two is the ideal scenario. The key to making your garden as attractive as possible is to provide as many feeding options as possible and to use 'native' as the buzzword when it comes to stocking your garden with plants. That said, some of the best wildlife garden plants are actually not native to Britain. Perhaps the best known is that urban invader, the Buddleja or 'butterfly bush'. It is incredible to see the number of butterflies and other insects that this plant can sometimes attract. I have stopped in my tracks on many occasions while strolling down city streets just to marvel at the collection of butterflies adorning some random person's front garden. The fact that it is a night-scented plant means that is also great for moths, too.

Whatever the growing conditions within your garden, and irrespective of whether it's large or small, there will be plants to suit. Like us, plants are versatile, some species being able to thrive pretty much anywhere (although others can be moody about where they set root).

For successful gardening and easy maintenance be sure to match a plant's specific preference to each location within your garden. The problem is that there are just so many plants to choose from – at the last count there were at least 75,000 listed in the Royal Horticultural Society's *The Plant Finder*! However, the vast majority have little value for wildlife. Try to select plants with nectar- and pollen-rich flowers, as well as fruit- and berry-bearing shrubs and trees. Since different plants have different requirements, before making a choice bear in mind the amount of direct sunshine your garden receives and the soil type and its pH (its acidity or alkalinity). If you want to check the pH of your soil you can pick up an easy-to-use test kit at any reasonable garden centre for a couple of quid.

Garden borders have a year-round appeal, not only to us but to wildlife as well. Ideally, aim to establish a mixture of low maintenance plants that will provide colour during every season – great for lazy gardeners like me! To create a mixed border you should start with a permanent framework of larger shrubs and a few conifers – and if space permits, a tree or two. Species that will offer shelter and fruit for the birds, such as Hawthorn, Holly, Dog Rose and Goat Willow, are a good start. Think about planting Pyracantha 'Soleil d'Or', Cotoneaster 'Cornubia' (a favourite with thrushes and Waxwings) and rambling roses that will produce lots of rosehips such as the white, single flowered Rosa 'Pleine de Grâce'. Blend evergreens with deciduous shrubs and select plants that add colour during each season. Infill with herbaceous perennials, ornamental grasses, small shrubs, heathers and herbs and fill any gaps with short-lived annuals and biennials for bursts of seasonal flower.

Kids love growing Sunflowers and get a real Jack and the Beanstalk buzz as they watch the seedlings they have planted grow to great heights. The birds and bees will love them too, so it is always worth adding a few into the mix. Plant bulbs to grow through ground-cover plants and lawns, and under large deciduous shrubs. Bulbs and early spring-flowering shrubs, such as Mahonia, Winter Jasmine and heathers will provide a nectar source for

Buddleja

early emerging bumblebees and other insects – I have even watched Blackcaps sampling the nectar from Mahonia flowers. Climbers such as Wisteria, Honeysuckle and Clematis are always good, too. Grow them through established shrubs and trees for cascades of extra blooms. Ivy is another great climber that is valuable for wildlife, providing pollen and nectar for insects such as bumblebees, nesting sites for birds and roosting spots for bats. Its berries are also an excellent food source for birds during the winter. Try to avoid the classic autumn clear-up as seed heads provide a food source for wildlife, and dead, hollow stems a vital home for insects to overwinter in safety. Instead, delay cutting back the dead stems of perennials and ornamental grasses until around March.

If you are lucky enough to have a large lawn it is always worth dotting a few Bird Cherry trees around it. However, if you have a smaller garden, planting a Crab Apple is another option. Buckthorn and Alder Buckthorn are both native shrubs that can grow in most garden soils and are also a must, not least because they are the only food plants for the caterpillars of the Brimstone butterfly. Establishing shade-loving plants and bulbs under large shrubs and trees to create a woodland floor effect will attract birds that prefer to forage on the ground. You could also consider creating mini-habitats such as leaf, twig and log piles at the back of a border, out of site. In fact, good log piles can be a fantastic draw for many invertebrates and if you live in southern England could provide a home for the endangered Stag Beetle and its larvae.

If you have the space, keeping a wild patch in your garden is always a good idea, since one man's weed is a bird's insect heaven. Allowing an area of grass to grow long is essential for egg-laying insects like butterflies, many of which also love weeds like nettles. Think about introducing some Teasel to see if you can tempt in a roving flock of Goldfinches that just love feeding on the spiky seed heads during the autumn.

And finally, on a non-birdy note, think about starting a compost heap. As well as being a great source of nutrients for your garden, these provide a warm home for a whole host of creatures, including amphibians and reptiles. Along with log piles, they also provide vital shelter for our diminishing population of that old garden favourite, the Hedgehog.

Blackbird (male) feeding on *Cotoneaster cornubia* berries

Ponds, bog gardens and small water features

Ponds

Ponds, as well as being a beautiful feature of any garden, especially if they are well maintained, can potentially attract in a great variety of wildlife including birds that will come to drink and bathe. I remember digging a pond in my back garden during a period of teenage angst. In fact, this was against my parents' wishes, and I dug the hole behind their backs. My aim was to create a habitat for ducks and my own colony of frogs, but in digging the pond I forgot one crucial factor – I needed to line it to hold the water in. So, until it completely dried up, I was left with a boggy, putrid marsh with no ducks or frogs, but instead the temporary home to a multitude of mosquito larvae!

The great thing about a pond is that it can be any size or shape you wish. As I discovered, keeping the water in is clearly important, but you can just simply place a sink or half a barrel into the ground and fill it up. For a healthy, low-maintenance pond you should ideally choose a location in the garden that gets sunlight in the morning and at least some shade in the afternoon. Avoid siting it under the overhanging branches of a tree otherwise you will

forever be raking out leaves, and the roots of the tree may eventually pierce the pond's lining. It is best to position your pond in a spot where you can easily watch the goings-on from the comfort of your living room sofa. When designing a pond, it is important to provide a slope on at least one side to allow visiting birds and other wildlife ready access to the water; this also provides an easy means of escape should anything fall in. Try to ensure that the water depth in part of the pond is at least 60 cm so that amphibians and invertebrates can overwinter without freezing solid, and maintain lots of shallow areas less than 30 cm deep for marginal plants to establish.

Populate your pond with a range of aquatic plants and don't wait for them to arrive naturally, as that could take years. Plant wildlife-friendly flora around your pond and try to link it to the existing vegetation in your garden to create mini wildlife corridors between the habitats. Never introduce invasive species, particularly those banned from sale, such as New Zealand Pygmyweed, as these can spread quickly and effectively clog up your pond. Despite the popular notion that transferring water from an existing pond will help to populate yours with life, doing so could actually spread disease and introduce unwanted flora. I would advise letting the wildlife come to your pond naturally, since there is no real need to give it a kick-start. When filling or topping up your pond it is far preferable to use rainwater, for example from a water butt, rather than tap water, which, as it contains chlorine, nitrogen and phosphorus, is not ideal for wildlife and can result in blooms of algae developing. If you want your pond to be a wildlife pond don't stock it with ornamental fishes, as these love to dine on tadpoles and invertebrates and can create a rather sterile environment.

It is important to remember that ponds can be hazardous if you have small children around – as they just love poking about in them. There are ways of reducing the risks, such as by covering small ponds with a metal grid or fencing off larger ponds and fitting a childproof gate, but, as anywhere, make sure that kids are supervised at all times whenever they are playing around near water.

Bog gardens

Bog gardens are a safer option than ponds if you have small children frequently playing in the garden. They are essentially areas of permanently wet ground and can be particularly suitable for smaller gardens, although also valuable for wildlife as extensions to larger ponds. There are plenty of gorgeous plants that do not thrive in open water but love the conditions

Common Toad

provided by a bog garden. Try establishing Purple Loosestrife, Marsh Marigold and Water Mint. To avoid your bog garden drying out too quickly, you should aim to create a reasonably large area and construct it as you would a pond – only much shallower. It is, however, good to puncture the liner to allow for some drainage. If you have very limited space creating a bog garden using a shallow container might be your best option.

Small water features

Whatever the size of your garden, you can always provide a water feature that will quickly become a refuge for wildlife. Large plastic plant pots can be turned into great water features, but even a small planter trough will do the job. Should your container have pre-drilled drainage holes you should line it first with a sheet of butyl rubber. Then add a layer of gravel at the bottom and insert an upturned brick or inverted plant pot to create a shallow area or ledge where birds can stand to drink or bathe without fear of drowning. You could also introduce a planted basket of marginal plants with the top at or just below the water's surface. Try to position any water feature so that it is sheltered from prevailing winds and, in order to minimize evaporation, not exposed to direct sunlight for long periods.

+++

As you'll have seen, there's a great deal you can do in an urban garden to encourage birds and other wildlife to visit or take up residence. The next step is to enjoy watching the results, and the following section provides an overview of the equipment and other tools you might find useful in enjoying the fruits of your efforts that much more.

Great Tit

TOOLS OF THE TRADE

As you will soon discover, Britain's towns and cities are filled with gorgeous-looking birds. However, even those with muted, subtle colours have a lot of beauty about them. Close examination of a male House Sparrow, for instance, will show that it is not just a brown, featureless small bird but instead an intricately plumaged grey, brown and white beauty. Some of the birds that you will see in your garden or local area will be instantly recognizable – but others will totally defy identification. Or so it may seem. Hopefully, you will have been trying to make basic notes on the unidentified birds that you find on your travels, and intently watching the birds that you do know to learn more about their habits and plumages.

A lot of the information that you garner while you are watching birds will be subliminal. Many garden birders I know can tell immediately that a Blue Tit is at their feeder even from the briefest of views. This comes down to a familiarity that results from hours of observation, even though the garden birders concerned do not realize that they are putting in the hours. This is part of the secret of birding. Whenever people remark "how did you recognize that from a mile off," the subtitled answer is quite simple: by putting in the time. Although this might sound like a chore, it is anything but. I think watching birds is one of the most liberating and wondrous things that you can do with your clothes on, and with each passing second you will be learning more and more. Eventually, after watching enough Starlings flying overhead, for example, you will unknowingly wake one morning being able to instantly recognize that species' triangular silhouette, however brief your sighting.

Birding is all about looking closely at every bird that you see, even if you think you know what it is. It may be a familiar species displaying an aspect of behaviour that you have never seen before, or be in a plumage with which you are unfamiliar. Sometimes you may find that it was not the bird you thought it was in the first place but something completely different. I learnt that lesson very early on and now try hard to ensure that I don't take anything for granted.

Bird books

You will need help in order to achieve the level of subconscious Zen that experienced birders exhibit, and the first step will be to buy a field guide that covers the birds you are most likely to encounter. If you're just starting out, one that only covers British birds would be ideal. Having said that, my first field guide was one that also covered species found in remote corners of Europe and North Africa. It included birds that have never been recorded in Britain, and a good few that I still haven't seen anywhere. So, unless you are a birdnut like I was who wants to learn everything about every bird, I suggest leaving that kind of tome for a later date.

Guides of sorts to British birds have been with us for hundreds of years. The first bird book was published in 1544 by scholar and clergyman William Turner, a man now dubbed the Father of British Ornithology. His book *A Short And Succinct History Of The Principal Birds Noticed By Pliny And Aristotle* certainly didn't have a short and succinct title! It was

No field guide depicts a Black Redstart sitting like this.

written in Latin and contained information on many species that had not previously been described as British birds. It was hardly a field guide but it was the book that launched a thousand ships. The first modern field guide came in 1934, born in America courtesy of ornithologist, bird artist and legend, Roger Tory Peterson. He had the bright idea of painting colour plates featuring similar-looking birds together and annotating them with arrows pointing out the differences. This simple adaptation on a theme changed the look, design and approach of field guides forever. Genius!

The thing to remember about field guides is that they are just that – guides. They are a compilation of interpretations of what particular species generally look like in certain given plumages. Usually, each species is illustrated in its male, female, immature/juvenile, breeding and non-breeding guises. As a youngster I thought that the birds depicted in my book were exactly what I would expect to see. So confusion reigned when I started finding things that were not in the book. Although within a species, birds of the same sex and/or age generally look the same, they can still sometimes display a heck of a lot of variation. Blackbirds are a good example. Most males look identical but some may have varying amounts of white in their plumage – something that no book could ever cover in full.

Every birder, whether a novice or a world expert, needs to use field guides. However, field guides do have a slight stigma attached, as some experienced birders believe that they have no need to carry one about as doing so might suggest a lack of knowledge. I even know people who have ripped off the front cover of their book in order for it to not be immediately recognized at a distance by their peers – how ridiculous and vain! There is no shame in pulling a book out in the field to look up a bird that you have just seen or want to learn more about. I habitually carry a field guide around with me and refer to it if need be. Nobody knows everything, even if they pretend to, and at the very least, producing a book – whether in printed form or as an app on your smartphone (which I will cover later) – can greatly speed up the identification of tricky species. The other advantage of carrying a field guide is

to be able to show other, less experienced birders or non-birding passersby the bird that you are looking at. This really is a great way of engaging with people.

Nip down to your local bookshop or look online to check out the range of identification books on offer. Choose one that you like the look of or, better still, ask your birding friends for recommendations or do some research on the Internet. Make sure that it covers the species found in the UK and that it has a range of easily referenced quality images that show the birds perched and in flight in a variety of plumages. Most field guides will also include distribution maps and these have a very important role to play in helping you to identify unusual species. By examining them you will, for example, have strong evidence that the female Whinchat you have just found feeding in an area of urban grassland in mid-December is far more likely to be a closely related female Stonechat. You will see that as the Whinchat is a summer visitor it should be sunning itself in Sub-Saharan Africa. Portability also has to be a consideration, as you will want to take the book around with you – and ideally it should slip easily into you coat pocket. It is a field guide, after all. Larger format books are great, too, although understandably will tend to lead a more sedentary life on a bookshelf or sat on a coffee table.

I am often asked whether field guides featuring artwork illustrations or photographs are best. Although things are changing with the advent of digital photography, traditionally I have had a preference for illustrated guides because species are normally arranged on a page in a way that allows easy comparison of their key identification features. You just need to bear in mind that the birds are not always depicted in a way that you are likely to see them in real life – not many pose perfectly in the open with their chests puffed up, for example. As lovely as many photographs are, they can be misleading due to the light in which they were taken or the nature of the background. A photograph also only reflects a fleeting moment in time, and rarely conveys the intricacies of all the plumage details in the standardized way that a series of illustrations can. That said, photographs are undeniably true to life and don't rely on an artist's interpretation. At the end of the day, it's best to check out the available options and choose the book that best suits your psyche.

It makes sense to try to learn the order in which the birds appear in your field guide. Nowadays, most guides start with the swans, geese and ducks and end with the buntings. This knowledge may come in handy if you need to refer to something quickly, although I guess that checking the index for the name of the bird you're after may actually not take that much longer. However, knowing that the raptors, for instance, are featured somewhere near the front, is likely to save valuable time by avoiding thumbing through the whole book.

Once you have your field guide you are likely to want to start visiting places away from home to catch up with species that are not normally found in your local area. There are quite a few 'where to watch' guides on the market that give detailed information on a host of different birding venues up and down the country. These books are either individual county guides or one-stop guides to the nation's top birding spots. At present, there are surprisingly few books on where to go urban birding in the UK, but that is something I hope will be addressed sooner rather than later.

Finally, as well as field guides, there is a proliferation of books available for all levels of experience and interests within the world of birds. This appears to be a steadily growing market, with ever more titles being published every year, seemingly unaffected by the reach of the Internet. This is probably because there's something very visceral about holding a book in your hands – and long may that feeling continue.

Birding magazines

Another element of a birder's life when it comes to printed media is magazines. Although seemingly a dying breed these days, especially in the face of the information freely available online, there are still two main bookstand publications – *Bird Watching* and *Birdwatch*

Blackbird

magazines. Both have their merits, so buy one of each and decide which best suits your needs. There are also the magazines that you receive by default through membership of organizations like the RSPB and the WWT, which often contain information that is very helpful to birders who are just starting out. Other titles are available on subscription only, such as the long-standing British Birds, although these publications tend to be aimed at experienced birders.

Binoculars

To make sense of the pictures and descriptions in your field guide, if you haven't done so already you may feel the need to graduate to the next level of being an urban birder by getting a pair of binoculars – a key tool of the trade. When I started birding I did it all with the naked eye, initially because I didn't realize that people used binoculars. Frankly, I didn't even know they existed. When I did make that revolutionary discovery, I couldn't afford a pair – and nor could my mum, until I pressured her into buying a pair on hire purchase. My birding life was transformed forever overnight and I now can't imagine life without a pair in my hands.

Binoculars have come a heck of a long way since their inception, and today an array of manufacturers producing a wide range of models, with prices to match. They have gone from resembling opera glasses and being called field glasses, or referred to as a 'set' of binoculars, to being dubbed as 'bins', 'binos' 'noculars', 'binocs' and 'goggles'. And, like cars,

people now refer to their binoculars as brands: "my pair of Leicas," "Opticrons," "Swaros" or "Zeiss." But with all this choice, which binocular (to use the correct term) is the right one for you? Should you spend a small fortune on supposed optical excellence or would a cheaper pair costing £40 suffice?

Firstly, think about what you will be using them for. Will they be spending their life on the windowsill only occasionally being called into action, or will they be a major part of your everyday life, being taken everywhere as you try to satisfy your insatiable quest to learn more about birds? A cheaper pair would be perfectly adequate for most urban garden birding, whereas a more robust and, ultimately, more expensive pair may be the thing to have if you are a budding urban explorer. Either way, to use another vehicular analogy, it is like buying a car: you have to find a model and price range that suits your preference and needs. Too often people shell out on really expensive binoculars that they rarely use, or, conversely, purchase an ultra-cheap pair, such as those so frequently advertised within the pages of the Sunday supplements, only to then wonder why they cannot see anything through them.

Once you have narrowed down your options, I would strongly advise trying out several pairs to see which suits you best. For urban birders, a local independent camera shop can be a good place to start your research. But if you visit one of the larger nature reserves out of town you will find that many now have optics shops staffed by knowledgeable people who will help you to make the right purchase.

Porro prism binocular   Roof prism binocular

But what exactly is a binocular? Well, ever since the invention of the telescope (an instrument to be considered later for the budding birder's armoury) in the 17th Century, putting two together side by side was almost immediately the natural progression. So binoculars are, in effect, portable twin-barrelled telescopes, each barrel containing glass elements called lenses and prisms. These catch, magnify and direct an image down the length of the barrel that falls as two pools of light upon the user's eyes. Most of the early binoculars used Galilean optics: they had concave eyepieces and, at the other end, convex objective lenses. An observer would have had had a narrow field of view and not much magnification – and they really were like looking through two empty toilet rolls! However, binoculars have come a long way since then and nowadays there are two basic types to choose from: Porro prism and roof prism.

Porro prism binoculars

In 1854, the Italian optician, Ignazio Porro, invented the prisms that bear his name. These prisms corrected the inverted image flaw, which was a major drawback to the binoculars of his day, and resulted in the classic 'offset' shape that most people think of when describing a binocular. Compared with roof prism binoculars in a similar price range, Porro prism binoculars provide a brighter image, as the light travels through them along a less complicated path. Another advantage of this type of binocular is that the distance between the two objective lenses – the ones at the bird end – tends to enhance the 3D effect for the viewer. However, although Porro prism binoculars are usually less expensive than roof prisms they are generally not as robust and more easily knocked out of alignment, resulting in a double image.

Roof prisms binoculars

Roof prism binoculars are designed around a rather more complex prism system than Porro prism binoculars, and thanks to improvements in modern optical engineering offer excellent image quality. They tend to be more ergonomically designed than Porro prism binoculars, and have a sleeker shape that lends itself better to birder-friendly features such as waterproofing and close-focussing. This has resulted in roof prism binoculars becoming the weapon of choice for many birders, albeit that they are generally considerably more expensive than Porro prisms.

So what exactly should you be looking for when choosing your binocular? The ideal is something light, sturdy, portable and weather resistant. As mentioned earlier, the quality of the glass and lenses is important in ensuring that you have a sharp image. The technical things to check are the field of view, which should be as wide as possible for scanning vistas; the depth of field, which needs to be sufficient to enable you to pick out birds through tangles of branches; the ability to focus close, which is especially useful in woodland situations; and an easy-to-use fast-focusing system. Not all of the binoculars that you pick up and look through will be able to deliver all of these attributes.

Make sure that your binoculars feel comfortable in your hands and that when you're looking through them your index finger lands comfortably on the focussing wheel that lies between the barrels. The binoculars should not be too heavy or bulky and should fit your face. But most importantly, make sure that you can see through them without straining your eyes. Years of watching too many James Bond movies as a kid made me believe that looking through a pair of binoculars involved seeing the world through a side-on figure-of-eight field of vision. Well, I can assure you that this should only happen on telly. If you cannot see a single round image, or if you are getting black patches or double vision then the binoculars are either not suited to you or have not been correctly set up. If you wear glasses be sure to fold or twist down the eyecups, the circular ring around the eyepiece, to help to achieve a full field of view. Indeed, spectacle wearers should look for binoculars with what is called long eye relief. Put as simply as possible, eye relief is the ideal distance that your eye should be from the eyepiece of the binoculars. If your eye is farther away from the eyepiece than the eye relief distance, then you will begin to lose the outer edge of the image. In other words, the farther your eye is from the eyepiece the smaller the field of view that you will see.

The weight of a pair of binoculars, as most people tend to refer to them (strictly speaking, of course, they are a binocular), is also an important consideration – anything over a kilo being more suited to muscle-bound behemoths. My original binoculars weighed a ton and felt like they were constructed from wrought iron. If I raised them too quickly I stood the chance of smacking myself in the face – which of course I unfortunately did on numerous occasions! In recent years, however, polycarbonates and lightweight metal alloys have increasingly been used in binocular construction and some of the most popular models for birding now weigh just 650–800 grammes. The fact remains, though, that most of the weight in quality binoculars can be attributed to the glass, so there are limits to how light they can become.

When out birding we subconsciously droop our neck after a period of time, particularly if we're wearing heavy binoculars, and this can lead to all sorts of aches and pains. However, shortening your binocular strap as much as possible can make a big difference. According to my friend Lee Saxby, an expert on natural locomotion and a movement coach, the shorter the strap the less likely it is that your neck will be pulled down. When he shortened the strap of my binoculars so that they sat on my sternum, as opposed to nestling on my belly, I almost immediately noticed an improvement in how I felt.

To alleviate both neck and back pain, many birders spread the weight of their binoculars by attaching them to a type of harness specially designed for the job. Another option is to carry your binoculars as an archer transports their quiver – slung over the shoulder and across the chest with the binoculars resting under one arm or even on your hip. Whichever way you prefer to support your binoculars, when holding them to your eyes try to get into the habit of tucking your elbows into your midriff for support. You may find this less tiring on your arms than holding your binoculars aloft with your elbows out to the side.

The type of strap on your binoculars can also affect how you feel after a day in the field. On older models it is often made of thin leather or plastic that can cut into your skin,

something that can become particularly uncomfortable on hot days when you're more likely to be sweaty and less likely to be wearing something around your neck – although even more modern straps with a broad, padded section can still rub. Also, if you're out birding in the sun you may end up with an uncool-looking pale stripe across the back of your otherwise tanned neck – something else that using a harness may help to prevent.

Another important issue to explore is how comfortable the binoculars feel in your hands. Make sure that the optics that you choose are a pleasure to hold: neither too heavy, nor too light. Women generally have smaller hands than men, so a smaller binocular can sometimes be more suitable. And smaller does not mean optically inferior, by the way. Unlike in the bad old days, size is not a measure of strength, as some binoculars, despite their small stature, have the same magnification as larger ones and have excellent light gathering capabilities. Compact binoculars are also a popular choice as a second pair to keep in the glove compartment of your car, or to be used by children starting out in birding. Their small size does, however, mean that they have small objective lenses, which in turn means that the image they produce is less bright.

I'm often asked how this magnification business works. Well, briefly, all binoculars are defined by two key numbers such as 8×42 or 10×50. The first number is the magnification and means that the Starling that you are looking at will appear to be, in these cases, eight or ten times closer than it actually is. The thing to remember, though, is that a larger magnification does not necessarily amount to better urban birding. This is because as the magnification goes up, image quality deteriorates due to the fact that less light is let through the lens and the field of view is reduced. Higher magnifications also amplify any handshake or unsteadiness. The other number is the diameter of the objective lens (the large end of the binoculars) in millimetres. This determines how much light can be gathered to form an image and directly affects performance; thus the larger the lens, the brighter the image. An 8×42 binocular will therefore look brighter than an 8×25, even though both enlarge the image by the same amount. Most birders go for 8× or 10× magnification when choosing a pair of binoculars. I find that it is sometimes difficult to notice the difference between the two, but 8× is generally the binocular of choice when it comes to woodland birding, whereas 10× is great for scanning reservoirs and skylines.

Generally, it is best to steer clear of zoom binoculars, since to my mind they are nothing but gimmicks with an optically poor performance to match. Image-stabilized binoculars are designed to minimize the effect of shaking, which is a great idea in theory. However, the few I have looked through were a little cumbersome and the image quality not that great. However, if you suffer from a neurological complaint this type of binocular could be very useful in giving you a stable image. Also, binoculars are more frequently becoming available in colours other than the classic black. That said, the vast majority of optics that I see wielded by birders, urban or otherwise, are still black, with a few green and occasionally tan coloured models added to the mix. In my view, less is more: pull out a pair of bling-bins in an urban area and you are more likely to find yourself targeted by the local villains.

Now that you have chosen a pair that you get on with, the next trick is to set them up to suit your eyes because, as mentioned earlier, you should never have to be straining in order to look through them. Everyone's eyes are different and we humans tend to have one dominant eye. The first thing to do is to adjust the distance between the eyepieces in order for the binocular to fit comfortably on your face. This is easy to do as binoculars are hinged. You will need to be able to look through both lenses in order to see a single image. If ever you get black areas or can only see through one eye it means that the eyepieces have not been set properly for your face.

Binoculars are made so that you can focus one eyepiece independently from the main focusing column allowing for each eye to be equally balanced. Check out which eyepiece is the adjustable one known as the diopter: normally it's the one on the right and has a series of numbers around its rim. If it is the right eyepiece, then cover the right barrel with the palm of your hand and, looking through the left eyepiece with your left eye, focus on an object around 20 metres away using the main central focusing knob. It is important not to close your right eye during this process, because your brain will know you have closed your eye and will immediately compensate with your left eye. When you are happy with the sharpness, uncover the right barrel and cover the left, and look with your right eye through the right eyepiece. Things may look a little blurry. With some binoculars you will need to "unlock" the diopter by tugging on the eyepiece for it to extend slightly. Then fine-tune the image you see by twiddling with the diopter until the image through your right eye is perfectly sharp. Lock the diopter by pushing it down and then look through your binoculars with both eyes – you should have an excellent single image suiting both eyes. Note that on some models the diopter is part of the central focusing barrel. You will need to go through the aforementioned steps but pulling the central barrel to release the diopter control instead. You are now ready to rock!

Modern binoculars are far sturdier than those of yesteryear. I remember birding friends of mine in the 1980s, with their prehistoric pairs, getting caught out in heavy rain or splashed by salt water while seawatching on some exposed headland. Unfortunately, their binoculars were never the same again, as water had seeped in, resulting in murky looking images. That situation is now, thankfully, largely a thing of the past. A few years ago, I was walking in my

flip-flops and shorts on a crowded Thai beach with my binoculars proudly around my neck. It was the first day of a holiday with my then girlfriend and I made the mistake of buying some chicken drumsticks from a beach vendor. Within minutes I was surrounded by a pack of dogs, all eager for a bite of my chicken. Perturbed, I ventured into the sea thinking that they would not follow me, but they did. So I clambered onto a rock, in full view of dozens of sunbathers. As I did so, my flip-flops slipped on the slimy seaweed and I fell into two feet of water. My binoculars were completely submerged, as was my pocket camera, and the chicken went everywhere, creating a feeding frenzy. Completely embarrassed, I scrambled out of the sea and scurried off to another part of the beach, out of sight. My camera was ruined but once I had wiped the sand and seaweed from my binoculars I found that they worked perfectly, none the worse for the experience.

Which brings me neatly onto maintenance. Despite their resilience, you still have to take care when cleaning your binoculars. Use a soft cloth specifically designed for wiping lenses and always blow away any grit before you start. Normal tissues should not be used as they leave behind tiny particles and are often impregnated with chemicals that may damage the coating of your lenses. Never try to dismantle your binoculars – this is a job best left to the professionals!

Once you are all set up, with your binoculars calibrated, you are ready to hit the streets and the nearest park in search of birds. It is a common misconception that you can pick up a pair of binoculars and master them straight away. I have often handed my binoculars to someone to show them a bird that I had discovered, only to see them fumble, unable to find the Reed Bunting that I have pointed out. Spotting and following a bird in flight with your naked eye is one thing, but brandishing a pair of binoculars and tracing an erratically moving bird is much more difficult than it appears. There is definitely an art to it. Even trying to spot a stationary Reed Bunting sitting in a bush fairly nearby can be tricky for a novice binocular user.

As a kid, I unwittingly practised hand-to-eye coordination using my binoculars. I used to stand in my back garden trying to get onto and follow everything that flew past. Initially, I managed to catch sight of only a few of the birds I sought. But gradually I taught myself to master the art of using binoculars by locating an object with my naked eye, working out exactly where it was, and only then searching for it using my optics. I started with relatively slow-moving jumbo jets before moving onto slightly faster-moving gulls. Starlings were next and before I knew it I could even track fast-moving Swifts!

I am not suggesting that you follow the same regime as I did, but it is a good idea to practise using your binoculars as much as possible. Whether it is a Blue Tit foraging in a rose bush, a Blackbird hopping over some mown grassland or Black-headed Gulls coasting over a park pond, watch them through your binoculars. You will soon learn how certain species move around and will eventually become adept at picking them up. Even though I have been birding for many years, to this day I still practise trying to locate birds. I often watch Swallows swooping and swirling around and try to follow their every unpredictable twist and turn. It is a great workout that will come in handy come the day a flighty rarity shows up. At the very least, continually looking at birds through your binoculars will aid your identification skills, regardless of how often you normally see them.

Telescopes

The next step in your natural progression to becoming an urban birder extraordinaire might be the acquisition of a telescope. But the first question to ask yourself is do you really need one. Ownership is often wrongly seen as a symbol of seriousness in the birding world, and it's important not to get sucked into thinking that anyone brandishing top-of-the-range optics is an ornithological guru. I know brilliant birders who are out there without either binoculars or telescopes, and at the other end of the scale people who hide behind expensive kit, pretending to be experts. And, of course, you will also have to bear in mind that in order to use your telescope effectively you will need to invest in a decent tripod – and be prepared to cart it all around.

Think of it like this: you could carry on birding quite easily with only a pair of binoculars but it would be very difficult if you just had a telescope. I spent the first 15 years of my birding life without a scope, although to be honest this was not out of choice. I totally lusted after one but financial restrictions kept ownership to just a pipe dream. Despite that, my birding was not enormously curtailed. Although I do now have a telescope I rarely use it in my everyday birding. In fact, in 20 years I have only employed it twice at my local patch. This is mainly because my day-to-day birding doesn't usually involve long-distance identification. To be honest, though, I generally cannot be bothered to lug it around on the off-chance that I might use it. That said, when it is called into action I instantly fall back in love with it and rue the days when I leave it at home. On one such occasion I was counting a group of Meadow Pipits flying around the grassland area at The Scrubs when I suddenly noticed a much larger pipit. Heart racing, I quickly realized that I had stumbled across something really interesting. If I had had my telescope with me, I would have quickly confirmed that my large pipit was indeed a rare Richard's Pipit from Siberia. Instead, I spent the best part of four hours trying to get close enough to view it through binoculars in order to distinguish its salient identification features.

Although scopes can be a good back-up for everyday birding, where they really come into their own is when you are sifting through ducks or gulls bobbing on choppy waves at your local reservoir, or scanning the shoreline looking for waders. However, my advice is this: only get a telescope when you really feel as though you want to take your birding to the next level.

As with binoculars, telescopes have come a long way since the days of Captain Hook and his drawtube. Modern telescopes, or scopes as they are affectionately known, are optically amazing by comparison, and take over where binoculars left off. They can help to bring your subject a lot, lot closer, especially when you're trying to watch a speck on the horizon, or enable you to really appreciate the plumage details on a distant Kestrel sitting on an open branch near the top of a poplar tree.

There are two basic styles of telescope: straight and angled. The former is effectively a long tube with the eyepiece at the narrow end. In the latter, the narrow end is angled upwards, meaning that you have to look down through the eyepiece to see anything – which takes a bit of getting used to. Angled scopes are comfortable to use outside when using a tripod, and are great for sharing with other people who can simply lean over to look through it; straight scopes often require the height of the tripod to be adjusted for shorter people. Straight scopes are often considered to be preferable when you are sitting in a hide or need to find a subject that has taken your interest quickly.

Many telescopes have interchangeable eyepieces that allow you to use lenses of different magnifications – such as 25× or 50× – whereas other telescopes have zoom lenses that, for example, can range from 15× to 60×. Zoom lenses work far better

Tripod (with legs folded away)

175

on scopes than they do on binoculars, but the higher the magnification the less bright the image will be. As with binoculars, it is important to check out the size of the objective lens when considering a potential scope. The clue is often in the name, as most manufacturers put the diameter (in millimetres) of the lens somewhere in the name of the product. The mechanics of the lenses work in a similar way to binoculars, but once you get above an objective lens size of 100mm you will start to need arm and shoulder muscles comparable to Arnie Schwarzenegger in his heyday in order to carry the scope around!

Whilst researching which scope to buy you may notice some with the term 'ED' printed on them; this stands for Extra-low Dispersion. When light passes through the various prisms and lenses in a scope the different colours that make up the image can get 'split', resulting in colour fringing and lower contrast. Using ED glass in the objective lens reduces these effects, but this type of glass is more expensive than regular glass. However, it is worth bearing in mind that at magnifications of 30× or lower, the benefits of ED glass are negligible.

A telescope really is only as good as the tripod on which it's mounted and choosing the best one to buy is therefore very important. Cheap, super-light tripods are likely to buckle at the first gust of strong wind, whilst others are far too heavy and more suited to propping up a Walrus. Once again, this is a classic case of trying before buying, and asking the following questions. Are the legs easy to extend? Do you need a degree in physics to attach the telescope to the head? Are the clips on the legs likely to jam fingers on cold, wintry days? A tripod for birding should also be sturdy enough to keep the scope steady in a gale, but light enough for easy transportation. The best models tend to be those constructed using carbon fibre – a very strong, durable material that is also very light – but these, unsurprisingly, are not the cheapest.

Birding using a telescope and tripod will sometimes mean walking around for hours in the field with it balanced on your shoulder like a rifle. After a while this can start to take its toll, and many birders develop 'tripod shoulder', localized pain resulting from the tripod digging into their shoulder for too long, even if the legs are cushioned. I have actually heard of birders having to result to shoulder surgery due to excessive scope and tripod use! To alleviate the problem you could consider buying a specially designed, lightweight flat backpack that distributes the weight of the scope and tripod across your back. The main downside of this type of backpack is that they do not have room for any other essentials you might need, such as your lunch, flask of tea, bird guide or camera.

Whichever way you decide to carry your scope, it is very important to make sure that it is securely fastened to the head of the tripod. You might get away with the scope falling onto a spongy lawn, but it's not likely to be a pretty sight if it crashes down onto concrete. Broadly speaking, there are two types of tripod head: fluid heads, and twist-and-lock heads. Fluid heads, as their name suggests, contain a fluid that reduces any jerkiness or vibration when panning or tilting, facilitating extremely smooth, free movement. These heads can make your tripod a joy to use because after moving your scope with the control arm, you can theoretically let go and the scope will stay where it is. A twist-and-lock head has a simpler mechanism that locks the head in place by twisting the control arm. They are usually cheaper than fluid heads but are prone to moving without being fully locked, which can damage the mechanism and ultimately result in heartache.

Both of these types of tripod head can have a quick-release system that involves screwing a plate to the base of the scope that locks into a slot in the top of the head. This is great for quick loading and unloading and there is usually a safety clip of some sort that prevents accidental dismounts. The best plates to use are those that have a sliding mechanism that enables the position of your scope to be adjusted so that it is perfectly balanced. This is particularly useful with a fluid head arrangement or if you add a camera or phone to the back of the scope and therefore change the centre of gravity.

As with choosing binoculars, take your time in picking the right scope. Do try out various models before buying and avoid the temptation to purchase cheap spotting scopes from the back pages of a Sunday supplement. Prices can range from £250 to over £3,000, so be wise and consider your purchase as a long-term investment. It is always worth speaking to other birders about their scopes and, indeed, taking a peek through as many varieties as possible before making the final decision.

Once you have got your scope, you will then have to learn how to use it! Although finding birds through binoculars can be difficult at first, spotting something through your scope may be even harder – particularly if you are trying to follow a moving bird. The key to proficiency when using a scope is to practise, practise, practise. The best approach is to find something of interest through your binoculars, and, only then, to try to find the same thing using your scope. Always start by using your scope at its lowest magnification, as this will give you the widest possible field of view and increase your chances of locating what you are trying to find quickly. The zoom should only be used once the subject you are looking for is in focus.

Finally, as I said earlier, before you make that commitment to buying a scope, it makes sense to weigh up carefully whether you really do need it. Will you use it regularly or will it be just a luxury item for special occasions. I have several urban birder friends who purchased telescopes and then left them to gather dust, unused. Scopes are not essential for most urban birding situations and you can always peer through somebody else's if the need arises!

Cameras

The camera is perhaps the ultimate piece of birding equipment. Although many of us would not relish the thought of lugging a huge camera around all day, we all envy the pin sharp results that are liberally plastered across social media and the magazines we read. But I believe that once you pick up a camera with the intention of taking pictures of wildlife you will have reached a crossroads where a decision will have to be made at some point. Are you a birder with a camera or are you a wildlife photographer? In my experience, most birders are happy if they can take good record shots of the birds they see, so in this section I am simply going to cover the basics of choosing and using a camera. Frankly, I'm not the best person to provide the detailed advice needed if you aspire to become a superstar as an award-winning wildlife photographer!

The advent of digital cameras has enabled many more of us to be brave and attempt to take pictures of birds. Prior to the revolution that was the invention of the digital point-and-shoot, taking a camera out in the field was the preserve of professional wildlife photographers or ultra-keen amateurs who understood the ins and outs of the art. Wildlife photographers tend to be a different species from birders, often owning very expensive kit and being ever keen to get that one-off, amazing shot. Some are clearly naturalists of the highest order, producing astounding work: they have studied fieldcraft to the nth degree and are quite happy to sit in a freezing hide for 18 hours to catch a rare moment. Meanwhile, others are only interested in a few target species, which they seek at the expense of other perhaps less gaudy-looking examples of bird kind.

Most birders with a camera are happy to photograph pretty much any of the birds they come across on their travels. On the other hand, I have often watched pros pick up their cameras only if the light is good or if their quarry is doing something particularly interesting. Although it may seem that there is often a straight toss up between lugging heavy camera kit around or balancing a tripod and telescope on your shoulder, there is an alternative – to cut corners by using 'bridge cameras' or indulging in digiscoping or phonescoping, all of which are covered a little later.

Whichever option you choose for capturing an image, it's always sensible to look carefully at the bird that you've discovered before trying to take a picture – either with your naked eye or through your binoculars. All too often, while fiddling around getting your camera ready, the bird in question will be long gone without your having had a chance to look at it properly.

A professional hide setup

The types of camera

There are essentially four broad types of camera: point-and-shoot, bridge, Digital Single-Lens Reflex (DSLRs) and Compact System Cameras. These can all be used for taking photos of birds, although each type has its pros and cons.

Point-and-shoot (or compact) cameras

As the name suggests, this is perhaps the most 'basic' type of camera system that you can purchase – although the term 'basic' is in fact entirely inappropriate, as these cameras, also popularly known as compact cameras, are capable of producing stunning pictures. Most use focus-free lenses or have an autofocus capability and automatically set the exposure options and turn on a built-in flash when needed. It's amazing to think that you can get all of these functions for often under £200.

The disadvantage of this type of camera for the urban birder is that they aren't much use unless the bird is practically sitting on your knee; they are really designed for recording family gatherings, taking holiday snaps and obtaining basic scenic shots. In the past, enterprising birders used to try to line up the lens of their camera with the field of view through their telescope in the hope of getting some sort of image – the results of which were often much more miss than hit. Soon, people began to fashion makeshift connectors in order to mount their point-and-shoots onto their telescopes more successfully. Recognizing this new trend, the optics companies were quick to invent tailor-made connectors that enabled point-and-shoot cameras to be fixed to their telescopes. Thus, digiscoping was born – but more about that a little later.…

Bridge cameras

These are the halfway house between point-and-shoot cameras and DSLRs and, pound for pound, pack a mighty punch. They are literally halfway between the two because the smallest models are only a tad bigger than the largest compacts, whilst the largest models are comparable in size and weight to the smallest DSLRs. However, at the time of writing bridge cameras do not have interchangeable lenses. They are the most popular camera system amongst birders, due to their zoom capabilities, the great images they capture, and their portable size and reasonable price (from under £200 to £1,000). With a good bridge camera

Point-and-shoot (or compact) camera

Bridge camera

it is possible to obtain fairly decent shots of distant birds using the telephoto zoom facility that can commonly reach a magnification of 10 or 20 times.

Bridge cameras are perfect for urban birding as they can be tucked into handbags and man-bags and often provide more than adequate images even if they are taken using the auto function.

Digital Single-Lens Reflex cameras (DSLRs)

This commonly used acronym, although widely recognized, is one that in a pub quiz, or worse still under the studio spotlights on Pointless, you would struggle to remember what the letters stood for. Digital Single-Lens Reflex cameras are the ultimate for any serious would-be bird photographer – amateur or otherwise. Technically, a DSLR is a digital camera that blends the optics and the mechanisms of the mirror and prism system – the single-lens reflex bit – with a digital imaging sensor (which has now all but replaced photographic film).

To the rest of us, DSLRs are simply the big bruisers with massive camo-flecked covered lenses that we see birders humping around nature reserves. They have largely replaced film-based SLRs and are lusted after by many because the images obtained with these cameras can be astounding – once you've mastered using it, since at first sight, the array of buttons and settings can be slightly disconcerting. Unlike with bridge cameras, setting a DSLR on auto is not really an option, so unless you really want to take your photography on a few notches it's probably best to master a bridge camera first. Ownership of one of these beasts is a commitment financially as well as technically. Camera bodies can cost £1,000s and the lenses sometimes more than a small second-hand car! They are also difficult to conceal when birding in urban areas frequented by shady characters who might be interested in its resale value.

Compact System Cameras (CSCs) (or mirrorless cameras)

Like DSLRs, Compact System Cameras have interchangeable lenses, but differ in not having a mirror and prism system to view the image. Instead, they have a built-in digital screen that shows pretty much what the photo will look like when you press the shutter button. CSCs and their lenses are a fraction of the size and weight of equivalent DSLRs and lenses, and considerably less expensive. This, plus the fact that the image quality is also very good, means that they're becoming increasingly popular for bird photography.

Digital Single-Lens Reflex camera (DSLR)   Compact System Camera (CSC)

As with binoculars and telescopes, it's always advisable to try before you buy. Ask around to find out what camera system is likely to be best for you. Try taking shots using cameras belonging to others and don't be afraid to go on a course or watch YouTube tutorials.

How to take a picture

Taking a picture can be as simple as setting a camera on automatic, pointing it at a bird and pressing the shutter. Or it could be far more complicated and involve considering the available light, the speed (or not) at which your subject is moving and the overall result that you want to achieve. Most of us start our amateur bird photographer life as we end it – with our camera firmly fixed on automatic. I certainly did for the first eight months of owning a bridge camera. I was petrified of accidentally setting it to some other configuration that would cause my images to have a sepia wash or some other disastrous effect.

Common Redstart. I love this shot even though it's rubbish!

The key things to remember when photographing birds

There is certainly some truth in the notion that you can buy the most expensive kit in the world, but you can't buy the eye. Don't be afraid of using your camera and take pictures all the time, even if you think it's the 'wrong' light or the bird is too distant. Never worry about making mistakes, since without trial and error you'll never learn how to take good images. You will soon discover the capabilities of your camera, but if from the very start you can remember a few basic pointers, your chances of taking that Facebook moment shot will be that much greater sooner rather than later. This will also help to reduce the time you have to spend sorting and binning!

▶ Make the most of good light but if it's sunny try to shift your position so that the sun is behind you – otherwise there's a fair chance that your photograph will be an overexposed silhouette. Although the best light conditions are generally early in the morning and late in the afternoon, you will often be faced with a dull, overcast day – but take the shot anyway as even in these conditions you can still get great shots.

▶ Think about the composition of your photo. A bird in its environment generally tells more of a story than an image of one filling the frame – less is often more.

▶ Capturing a bird's behaviour is more likely to result in an interesting image than a simple portrait. Your garden feeder can provide a great location for action shots, and your kitchen window can make an excellent hide.

▶ Avoid taking photos of birds against the sky, as the camera will often struggle to focus on the subject and give you the correct exposure unless you are able to adjust the settings quickly.

▶ If your subject stays still for long enough, click away and keep reviewing and subtly changing the focus and exposure settings to increase the likelihood of getting at least one great shot.

▶ When out and about, remember that your car can make a brilliant mobile hide, allowing you to get close to some birds.

▶ Seek advice from photographers with more experience. What they tell you might sound like double Dutch at first but gradually, like driving a car, changing your camera settings will become second nature.

▶ Always carry a spare battery and memory card in case you are 'caught short'.

▶ Finally, and most importantly, respect your subject. Never chase a bird or approach it too closely, as this is likely to cause it distress. Instead, allow the bird to approach you. Remember, the welfare of the bird is far more important than any photograph. Nest photography is a no-no, as it is illegal unless you have a special licence.

It goes without saying that bird photography, like all aspects of birding, should be fun – so keep pressing that shutter button! If you take enough pictures of the birds you see, you are bound to get some good images eventually. And learn to love the pictures you take, even if they are not pin-sharp or are off-centre – after all, they are your pictures and your memories.

The effect of vignetting

Digiscoping

Very simply speaking, digiscoping is the equivalent of using your telescope as a long lens on your compact camera or DSLR. It's important to note that not all cameras are suitable for digiscoping, so if you are interested in going along this route find out which models are compatible with your scope. Some telescope brands make specific recommendations as to the best cameras to use and even supply connectors, although in other cases you may need to buy a universal adapter. You can also now get connector hoods designed to attach DSLRs to a telescope.

When digiscoping you will have to ignore a lot of the conventional thinking on photography, as there are limitations. Forget about depth of field because what your camera records is what you see through the telescope. Also, digiscoping is really only suitable for static subjects, since tracking a moving bird and ensuring a sharp image is next to impossible. One of the main drawbacks is vignetting – when a dark circle appears around the central image. To overcome this you will need to zoom in on your subject using the telescope's zoom rather than the camera's. Using the camera's zoom will result in the image you take being much more fuzzy (technically termed pixelated) than had you cropped an image created by using the telescope's zoom.

Phonescoping

Taking photos with a smartphone is rapidly becoming as popular as digiscoping, especially given the exceptional lens quality now to be found in the higher-end models. Gone are the days when using your phone with a telescope involved clumsily trying to align the two, invariably resulting in a series of haphazard record shots. Now, with the aid of plastic adaptors that both fit your eyepiece and cradle your Android or iPhone, you can take some quite stunning imagery.

As with digiscoping, once you have your subject sitting still conveniently on the garden fence, you mount your phone using the adapter and, to reduce the vignetting, adjust the zoom on the telescope. Once the bird is roughly in focus gently touch the screen of the phone until the autofocus locks in. Sliding your finger up or down the screen will alternatively darken or lighten the general image. When you're happy with what you see, simply press the button as you would normally to take a picture. If you want to go a stage further and reduce blurring due to shake, just plug in your plastic cord headphones and simply depress the volume button, which will act as a remote shutter release.

A big advantage of phonescoping is that free apps, such as Snapseed, can be used in the field to process a picture, enabling you to tweet it out to the world very quickly. Alternatively, you can process images using the phone's in-built editing facility. Believe me, phonescoping is set to be a game-changer, especially as most of us now carry a mobile phone.

Video

Unless it's their profession, very few people go out specifically to record birds and other wildlife using purpose-built video cameras. It takes a lot of effort to film birds the way we see them in TV documentaries, and often involves the film-maker spending hours in a cramped, cold hide. However, practically all modern cameras and smartphones have a video function, which, for the urban birder, can be a very useful tool. Video can record subtle nuances in a bird's behaviour that photography would never capture, often making it easier to confirm its identification – and has the added advantage that you might also gain admirers on social media! So, when you're next confronted with a bird you don't recognize, or are fortunate enough to find or watch a rarity, why not switch your camera or smartphone to movie mode once you have taken some photos.

Both digiscoping and phonescoping are great for shooting video, even in slo-mo. However, the main disadvantage is that you are limited to what the telescope can pick up – so obtaining a video of a bird flying swiftly and erratically across a vista or overhead will be a step too far.

Storing your images

Digital photography has negated the need for expensive film processing and the physical storage of the resultant prints and slides. But, despite its convenience, it does have some drawbacks. The main thing that you have to plan for is storing the mass of digital information created every time you take a picture. Although you can save quite a few images

on your computer, ultimately this is not the answer, as your laptop's memory will soon be overloaded. You will therefore need to get into the habit of keeping your images on a portable external hard drive – small devices that can be obtained quite easily, even from some local supermarkets. Backing up your images onto a second hard drive or onto the cloud is always advisable, just in case the only hard drive you have is lost or fails.

Many people use programs such as Adobe Photoshop or Lightroom to process their images. This involves enhancing the colours and overall tone and contrast of the image, and improving its sharpness. This is a whole new world that in some cases can be quite time-consuming – although the results are generally worth the effort.

Sound recording

Recording bird sounds is an aspect of ornithology that has interested me ever since I was a youth. Learning about the work of early practitioners of the art, such as BBC sound recordist the late Eric Simms, and more recently giants of the trade like Chris Watson, who works a lot with David Attenborough, was fascinating.

Unfortunately, and particularly from an urban birder's perspective, we live in a very noisy world filled with the all-pervasive sounds of humanity. In order to become an urban birder you will therefore need to develop the ability to filter out some of that 'white noise' and become more receptive to bird song and calls – but how easy is it to record these sounds? It is possible to make recordings using a smartphone or by taking a video simply to record the sound. The problem is that you will have to be fairly close to the bird, and be prepared to record the wall of surrounding sound as well as the bird itself. However, with a directional microphone (or mic) it is possible to make some pretty decent recordings even in urban situations.

Perhaps the most interesting and illuminating recordings that you can make in urban areas are of night-flying migrants. There is a lot to be said for getting on an elevated rooftop during the dead of night when the city humdrum is at its quietest and pointing your microphone to the sky. According to Magnus Robb, sound recordist for The Sound Approach, urban areas often have more calling night-flying migrants than the surrounding countryside because the birds are attracted to, and indeed congregate near, the bright lights. To capture these sounds a parabolic microphone or a homemade flowerpot microphone will be essential. Recording equipment can be obtained quite cheaply, but the secret to success is to have a power-pack with a sufficiently long life that will keep the recorder going all night.

Recording bird sound using an improvised parabolic reflector!

Once you have the equipment and learnt how to use it, the next challenge is to understand how to decipher the sonograms (graphical representations of the songs or calls) etched onto the recorder's memory card. It is these data that enable you to specifically identify what you have recorded, as each species has it own graphic signatures. This, of course, takes time and requires some knowledge of the range of calls that each bird makes – but is a great way to learn.

The Internet

There have been three major milestones in the development of birding both here in the UK and across the rest of the world: the invention of the wheel, the advancement of optics and the birth of the Internet. It is the last of these innovations that has singularly changed the face of birding, birders and arguably even birds, forever. There can be few people out there who have not benefitted from the power of the Internet. Images of birds from all over the world are now watchable 24/7 alongside birding news and views. Information on any species, conservation issue, birding holiday or birding location can be called up within moments, and is constantly being updated. Interestingly, though, information regarding urban birding appears to still be in its infancy.

In the dim and distant days before Facebook, when the Internet was still in its shorts, forward-thinking birding pioneers were designing their first rudimentary websites, scribing the words for the first blogs and dreaming of podcasts. However, although the Internet has been with us in a mainstream way since the 1980s, it was initially shunned by most of the birders I knew, nearly all preferring the existing old-school modes of communication. Even large NGOs like the RSPB and the BTO had a negligible presence on the net. Things have moved on a thousandfold since then, and the virtual landscape has shifted and changed with it. Websites in particular have become increasingly sophisticated, and are now far more than just basic collations of information covering where to watch birds, rarity listings or academic studies.

Many of those pioneers and early adopters of the technology must have had an inkling that it was about to explode exponentially. Amongst the first of the major players in providing birding information in the UK was BirdGuides (now known as NatureGuides), who set about providing an up-to-the-minute listing of the rare and scarce birds that were currently being looked at – or for. This instantly made the possibility of going to look for an unusual bird – or twitching – a lot easier, since you could plan your day, on the day, thereby drastically reducing the chances of disappointment. I will discuss the phenomenon and obsession that is known as twitching in the next section.

Websites are now, more often than not, slick, targeted points of reference. There are still bloggers out there, but few update as frequently as they once did, perhaps finding it easier to tweet 240 characters or wax lyrical on their Facebook page. Fewer people or organizations indulge in podcasts, choosing now to broadcast video on social media sites such as YouTube.

News of a Ross's Gull turning up is likely to result in a major twitch.

The various social media platforms that include Facebook, Twitter and Instagram have made anyone and everyone capable of uploading whatever fact or conjecture they wish for the world to see and further disseminate. Using social media is a fantastic way to become acquainted with and follow, or be followed by, like-minded birders. However, as with any virtual society there is a dark side frequented by delinquent lowlifes who seek to debase others. The best advice is to block such individuals and to call them out if they are being overly offensive. In my view, the positive use of social media is a superb galvanizer of people. It has a very important role to play when it comes to citizen science by enabling participants to get involved in an easy and convenient way.

Webcams are another great development, allowing viewers from around the world to watch the minute–by-minute, albeit largely mundane, nesting activities of birds. Some of these live feeds are unbelievably popular. A great example is the footage of Peregrines nesting on Derby Cathedral, which has amassed in excess of four million views since 2007. Without the Internet many of these viewers would never have known about these birds. In fact, I would wager a bet that a substantial number had not even heard of a Peregrine prior to watching the feed. What I love about the birding world today is that it is now possible to form virtual bonds with other urban birders anywhere in the world. The Internet is still developing and in another ten years may be totally different from the way it appears today. But presently, in a society that demands everything on a plate in digestible chunks as of yesterday, is there a danger of us relying on technology too heavily and becoming lazy? Will the advent of the Internet and the general advancement of technology enhance us as birders? Only time will tell….

A Peregrine dining area with prey remains

Smartphones

Before the days of the Internet, information on birds was a lot harder to come by. There were far fewer magazines to read or books on the shelves to delve into, and we undoubtedly knew a heck of a lot less about birds then than we do now. During the dawn of twitching in the 50s and 60s, news of a rare straggler to our shores was spread either by the Royal Mail, when finders would alert other would-be observers by way of a postcard, or with a phone call if you were lucky enough to own a phone. In those days, if you weren't part of a grapevine then you would only hear about an interesting bird after it had long since disappeared.

I remember the days of going out birding and effectively being off the radar, with no means of contact until I saw a familiar red telephone box. In those days, if someone came across an unusual bird, they were invariably a million miles from any means of communication. Heart pounding, they would scan around frantically, looking for another birder to show the bird they had just sighted. Even if they did find a call box, they had to pray that it was working and could accept the 10p coins forced into the slot – assuming they had some loose change, of course. This was the scenario even in the middle of some urban

birding sites. To get any news out you would usually have to leave the area where you had been birding to go and look for a phone box – and in an urban area you stood more than a fair chance of finding a vandalized one.

Enter the mobile phone. We all know the story of the rise of the mobile, which started as a plaything of 80s yuppies and is now as universally owned as a set of keys. Who would have thought just 20 short years ago that mobile phones would now play such a big role in our daily lives? These days I feel almost naked if I have to walk the streets without one.

Most of us now own a smartphone. These gadgets are an incredible powerhouse that can allow us to stream live video onto social media, take photographs, record sound, track GPS coordinates, act as a satnav and, most importantly perhaps, make phone calls. Although texting used to be a big thing, with birders sending each other news of their findings, and often forming texting groups to inform each other of the latest bird news from a local patch or area, this activity is slowly being phased out by free apps like WhatsApp and Twitter. Regardless, if you frequent an urban patch already visited by other birders, try to get involved with a WhatsApp ring, or consider setting one up if there isn't one already, as this

Golden Oriole

is a great way to circulate news. There is barely anywhere in the UK without a mobile signal, so news of interesting birds can be communicated instantly.

Ironically, it is the phone call bit that can be the most annoying thing about mobile phones. All too often, when you're trying to spend a few quiet moments birding in an urban oasis, perhaps sitting in a hide, the peace is shattered by someone with a loud Eye Of The Tiger ringtone followed by an even louder one-way conversation. To minimize disturbance to both the wildlife and its watchers, perhaps having a more natural ringtone like the fluty song of a Golden Oriole or the warble of a Nightingale would be a good idea. The downside, though, may be that any birders present may suddenly freeze rigid thinking that they had just heard a major rarity!

Apps

The evolution of the smartphone has been a revelation for birders. Aside from all the great inbuilt features, you can download additional apps to aid your everyday birding. These fall into four main categories: field guides, identification guides, rarity alerters and citizen science apps.

Whole field guides can be downloaded onto your new shiny, sleek, all-singing, all-dancing device, allowing you not only to view the contents of the physical printed version of the book, but also to hear calls and songs and watch video clips. Some apps even allow you to compile lists of sightings and jot down notes. But, as with paper field guides, choose the app that you want to stick with carefully, as not all those available are that great. The ideal situation would be to get the app version of the book that you are already happy using. That way you will be familiar with the layout, and it is a perfect way of actually hearing the calls described in your electronic field guide.

Identification apps are to a large extent a hybrid of field guide and vocalization aid. At the cutting edge are the Shazams such as Merlin, which puts a name to that picture of a mystery bird you have taken, and Warblr that names the mystery calls and songs you have recorded. Both are ever-developing, with Merlin currently featuring mainly North American birds. One day soon, these, and other apps of their ilk, will really come to the fore. However, not all the identification apps available are really up to the job, so ask around for opinions before buying.

There are a couple of very good apps available that provide up-to-the-minute information on rarities – Rare Bird Alert and BirdGuides. These work on a subscription basis, that, simply translated, means the more you pay the more detailed information you get.

There are also a few cool data-entry apps, such as the BTO's BirdTrack and eBird that allow users to submit their sightings to databases, the aim of which is to build a more complete picture of the state of the populations of our birds. These apps also collate your personal lists and casual records for perusal whenever you wish. As important as these citizen science apps are, the main barrier they face is getting more people to change their birding habits by inputting data in the field. Over time, typing in data on the go will hopefully become second nature.

Finally, and perhaps of particular relevance to the readers of this book, there are a few site guide apps including *The Urban Birder City Guide* that points you in the right direction when it comes to finding urban birding sites.

BEING AN URBAN BIRDER

Having got the equipment you need to go birding, the next step is to go out there and really get stuck into your local patch or other urban birding site. Fieldcraft is a discipline that is as relevant in your local urban park as it is in a remote tract of countryside. The more you become stealthy in your approach to birding the more you will ultimately see. However, you do not have to go overboard. Just a few simple steps are needed in order to switch you from an urbanite to an urban birder in touch with your natural side. The first thing to think about is what to wear when you're birding.

Urban birding attire

"Do you wear a green anorak and hang around in bushes all day?" is a question I'm often asked by curious non-birding friends keen to understand why I find birding so fascinating. The cool thing about being an urban birder is that it presents a great opportunity to dispel this hackneyed image.

The advice that I will be offering on the clothing front will be largely common sense, and it is, of course, entirely up to you what you actually wear. So long as you indulge in layers in winter and are wearing clothing that doesn't rustle with every step, then you should be fine. Remember, functional is great but you can also do it with style. I once took a lady friend to Hyde Park on a winter's day to twitch two female Bearded Tits – the first to be recorded in inner London. We were amongst the throng, most of whom were wearing wellies, dark jeans, puffer jackets, thick woolly hats and gloves. Meanwhile, although my friend had binoculars around her neck, she was decked out in sexy high-heeled leather boots, fake fur coat and Cossack hat, and carried a Louis Vuitton bag. Certainly different from your usual birding attire, but it worked for her!

In the heart of our towns and cities, there's no need to dress as though you're prepared to be away in the wilderness for a few days, as there's always a nearby café to run into if you get caught in a heavy downpour. Let us ditch the need for tweed and a walking stick when watching garrulous Waxwings in your local supermarket car park on a wintry day. Neither is it necessary to be togged out from head to toe in green or full-on army camouflage flecktarn – the need to do so is negligible as many urban birds are used to the presence of humans. That said, sombre colours are generally considered to be best as they help you to blend in to the background; gaudy hues tend to beam out from the vegetation.

The key thing is to dress sensibly so that you can keep warm during the winter and cool in the summer. Stay dry and be prepared for the weather, remembering that it can be surprisingly cold first thing in the morning, even during the summer. Although you may be within an urban environment you are just as prone to be rained or snowed upon as your country birding counterpart. Even when visiting my local patch on a cold day I treat it as though I were on a nature reserve in Kent or the Grampians in Scotland, donning walking boots and a puffer jacket. Notwithstanding the heat island effect that is in play, when you're stationary for periods you will soon begin to feel the cold. I learnt that lesson the hard way after going on twitches away from the centre of London during the winter months as a young man, thinking I was cool in the gear that I had been wearing the night before at a club. Standing in plimsolls in snow at Beddington Farmlands in Surrey for two hours waiting for a rare Little Bunting to pop up made me appreciate the feeling of climbing Mount Everest in bare feet. The best clothing to wear for urban birding is actually quite straightforward, but I shall run through a few ideas on apparel.

Tops and jackets

Summertime birding fashion is quite easy, as you can simply sling on a t-shirt or shirt – but avoid garish colours that make you stand out. During the cooler days of autumn, and of course during the winter, out should come your long-sleeved tops, jumpers and fleeces. Be sure to wear several layers under your fleece, especially on very cold days to help retain your body heat. Jackets are obviously a must. During the summer I always pack a lightweight windproof and waterproof jacket in my backpack, in case our great British weather catches me out. Insulated jackets are essential during the winter as they offer great protection from the elements. Good quality garments tend to be quite expensive but they are well worth it – you can even be naked under some of these jackets and still feel toasty! My original jacket of choice was a parka that I bought from an army surplus shop in 1984 for the princely sum of £10. In terms of value-for-money, it was the best item of clothing I have ever purchased. It kept me warm during the coldest days, and lasted for over 20 years – and I still have it in reserve.

Bottoms

In terms of trousers, I am a great lover of jeans, but since they are not so good in the pouring rain, packing a pair of overtrousers is never a bad idea. However, if you feel a little cumbersome in two pairs of trousers, then why not try a nice pair of softshell pants over thermal underwear. During the summer there are very few things more liberating than decking out in shorts before heading off to do for some good urban birding. In most of our urban centres you will be largely free from the annoyance of tick bites that can result from walking through long grass.

Footwear

During the summer a pair of trainers will often suffice, especially if you're pounding the concrete streets in search of birds, and can be fine with other types of terrain provided the ground is not muddy. I personally prefer to wear a sturdy pair of boots throughout the

year, with either one or two pairs of socks, depending on the season. Check to make sure that they have a breathable lining to keep your feet warm and dry. Although Wellingtons are great for keeping water out, they are not so good at keeping the warmth in on chilly days and can make your feet sweaty in the heat.

Hats

Brimmed hats offer good protection against the sun and rain – but they don't have to look as if they were borrowed from Crocodile Dundee's wardrobe. There are many different styles available in several colours and you can often find them in good department stores. The key thing is to make sure that the one you get is weatherproof. I often wear a beanie or a baseball cap while out urban birding. Although the former is great during cold weather and the latter perfect for keeping the sun off my forehead and eyes, both are pretty useless in the rain. Again, weatherproof versions are available from all good outdoor gear stores.

Shades

It's certainly worth investing in a cool pair of shades. Shop around for a quality pair of sunglasses with break-resistant lenses that provide high levels of protection against ultraviolet light. It might sound trivial but as an urban birder you will be spending a lot of time outside looking up for passing birds of prey and the like. Sunglasses protect your eyes by cutting out the glare and enable you to view the sky without squinting.

Accessories

Now that you are fully togged up and ready to roll, the next thing you will need is something in which to transport all your changes of clothes, bird book, water and snacks. This is where a good backpack comes in: aim for one that's best suited to your size and needs, and, perhaps just as important, is weatherproof. This is not an item of equipment that you will necessarily find in one of the large supermarket chains, so pay a visit to an outdoor gear store. Although the colour doesn't really matter – green, blue, brown or mottled patterns are all fine – bright, florescent reds and yellows are a no-no, as they risk drawing attention to your presence.

Nuthatch

Fieldcraft

The first general rule of fieldcraft is always to consider the welfare of the birds that you are seeking. Try not to flush any bird unnecessarily, especially if it's a tired migrant, as repeated disturbance may prevent it from feeding and recuperating. For me, a birder's approach to fieldcraft should be the same in an urban environment as in a rural setting. As I've already mentioned, dressing in sombre colours and wearing rustle-free clothing can help to conceal your presence. When you're looking for birds try not to rush around noisily, and instead walk with slow, deliberate movements. I am not suggesting that you crouch down and move stealthily on all fours, as you are very likely to get funny looks, but a cautious approach can often bring the reward of sightings of birds you did not expect.

Having once tried to stalk some birds on all fours, with dire consequences, it is definitely something I will never do again. I was at Pak Thale, a superb area of saltpans and wetland habitats an hour south of Thailand's capital city Bangkok, on the trail of the now mega-rare Spoon-billed Sandpiper. I was super-excited at the prospect of seeing perhaps four of the 400 or so birds left in the world. Since there was no cover I decided to crawl 100 yards to get close to a bunch of waders that I suspected of containing a 'Spoonie' or two. This was in the blazing sun and involved crossing hard ground littered with sharp fragments – and I was wearing shorts. Around 40 minutes and two shredded knees later, I arrived at the spot. I peered over a small embankment that separated me from the waders that were now quite close. Almost immediately I was joined by a laughing Thai birder who had simply walked up at a normal birding pace without any of the waders even batting an eyelid!

There may be occasions when you're out birding and unexpectedly flush a mixed flock of birds that disperse into the nearby bushes. Resist heading in after them and instead wait a while to see if they return. As I mentioned earlier, birds often have circuits and once they've chilled out for a bit and accepted your presence, they may come back. It sometimes pays to stand still on the edge of a woodland clearing or area of scrub, or to sit unobtrusively by the edge of a reservoir or lake and just wait. By keeping still you begin to blend into the background and the local birds will start to accept you as part of the furniture – greatly improving your chances of having some really interesting close encounters. I tried this approach recently by just sitting quietly on a bench in a small park near the centre of Croydon in Surrey and waiting to see what happened. Behind me was a strip of thin woodland that bordered the whole park and after 15 minutes I was enjoying amazingly close views of foraging Nuthatches and Coal Tits.

On another memorable occasion, I was leaning up against a tree in a city wood in Helsinki, Finland and noticed a Great Tit nearby. It was aware of me too, but instead of flying away it became overcome by curiosity, approaching me closer and closer and eventually landing on my head momentarily before hopping onto a branch nearby. It repeated this behaviour several times before disappearing off into the wood. It was a very intimate experience and I felt privileged to have been the chosen one. I was just about to move when a Long-eared Owl flew in and landed in a tree on the edge of a glade a short distance away. Having perched there for a while, and not noticed me, it proceeded to quarter the glade looking for prey. It was one of the most amazing birding experiences I have ever had, and only because I stayed still in one spot for a period of time. Moments like these are certainly meditative; once you are relaxed you will find your mind wandering as you wait, listening to the sounds of nature all around you.

If you are waiting around in an area for a while, try to get closer to the ground by stooping, squatting, kneeling or sitting (it's always worth having something padded like a small cushion in your backpack just in case). If you decide to squat, there is a technique that's worth trying: go down onto your haunches with your feet flat and pointing outwards, and your knees apart; lean forward slightly with your elbows resting on your knees and push your bum out a touch to keep your back straight. This may sound complicated but it will feel quite comfortable and avoid putting any strain on your back. This is the way primitive

man used to rest while hunting, and how people still squat by the roadside in countries such as India and South Africa. I now do it all the time and it really is less tiring than standing.

Another great way to watch birds is to lie flat on your back. This can be particularly pleasurable on a warm summer's day in the long grass or even in a park – and you will be amazed at the number and variety of birds that may pass through your field of vision.

I have never understood why people habitually use loud, conversational voices while out birding. I have birded in the US as well as Eastern Europe and some of my hosts were almost bellowing at the top of their voices. Inside my head I am screaming, shut up! Although we still see birds, I'm always left wondering what we might have missed. I am from the old school and even though urban birds are probably used to hearing our chatter, I still think that being as quiet as you can is a good habit to get into. Similarly, when out with a group don't just assume that there are no birds around apart from the ones conveniently in front of the hide you're approaching. Birds are everywhere, so approach hides quietly watching for activity along the way.

Having said this, hides don't have to be like libraries – a low buzz of conversation is fine, especially when the talking is about getting people onto the birds that can be seen. The atmosphere might get a little tetchy though if arms with pointing fingers or telephoto lenses are suddenly thrust through the slats, startling any birds that happen to be nearby. When looking from a hide, never sit in ignorance and always ask for help if you are struggling to identify any of the birds. Most people will be only too pleased to assist, and at many reserves there will be local guides who are there specifically to point out the birds that can be seen.

One of the classic questions that birders ask each other is "is there anything around?" This is, of course, a very subjective question, as one person's bland bird is another's 'lifer' (a bird that you have not seen before). In my view there's no such answer as "nothing much" because even a Robin is interesting to watch. Also, when someone says there is nothing around, that may have been the case when they looked. But there might be something when *you* look. Remember, birds often do circuits and perhaps will have come back by the time you reach a particular spot – so whatever anyone tells you, always keep looking.

Occasionally, you may actually need to stalk a bird to get close enough to see its key identification features. Imagine the scenario: you're walking through an area of grassland and a small brown bird flushes in front of you and drops down again a few yards away. With a stealthy approach you will hopefully get prolonged views of your quarry on the ground, albeit probably watching you nervously – a Meadow Pipit in this case. Had you rushed in after it, the result would almost certainly have been the bird flying off again, leaving you with just a fleeting view of its tail end. That said, you should only stalk birds outside the breeding season in order to avoid any unnecessary disturbance to nesting birds or preventing adults from feeding their young.

Get into the habit of trying to remain inconspicuous by avoiding breaking the skyline – never stride boldly along the brows of hills and the tops of embankments, as any birds that you were likely to see will almost certainly have caught sight of you first and melted away. This is particularly important when you are birding in open vistas such as reservoir banks, grassland and shorelines. Walk below the brow and break the horizon cautiously, ideally in a crouched position. You may be forgiven for thinking that fieldcraft is a solo activity but it can be a group thing too, provided you keep noise to a minimum. I have many happy memories of being out with my mates looking for migrants in the autumn and splitting up so that we effectively covered more ground, regrouping whenever something interesting was found. This proved to be a very efficient way of searching for birds and invariably resulted in far more sightings than would have been the case if any of us had been birding alone.

Try to avoid breaking the skyline

202

Safety

You may have some concerns about the safety aspects of urban birding, but in all my years of poking around in towns and cities I've never encountered any problems wearing binoculars. As long as you're sensible and avoid renowned no-go areas you should be perfectly fine. The rise in the popularity of birding, and especially urban birding, means that bystanders will not view you with the scepticism that was once perhaps the case. Instead, you may be approached by inquisitive folk keen to know about the birds you are looking at. I would, though, be wary of walking around in known dicey areas waving expensive kit around, as there is no need to invite potential problems. So keep your wits about you, particularly after dark.

All this said, caution should be exercised especially if you are a lone woman birding in the early evening or exploring an ornithologically poorly known sector of an urban area. The simple rule is to avoid areas where you might be exposed to potential danger. Keep to the paths in such areas and, if you can, go with friends. If you do decide to go birding alone, let someone else know where you are headed, and if you are particularly concerned it's worth considering carrying a personal alarm.

A common sense rule, whether you are in an urban area or not is never to leave expensive optics on view in a parked car. Thieves often target birders' cars, knowing that their owners are often so excited about the birding to be had that they forget about the need for security.

Finally, you are asking for trouble if you trespass on private land or breach the security at gravel extraction sites or areas with dangerous working machinery.

Usually, the only annoyances you could expect to face while out urban birding are being barked at by dogs or being hit by the occasional stray football. Over the years, I have been woofed at by thousands of dogs, most of which were just over-exuberant animals. However, I was once attacked and bitten on the arm by an out-of-control Pit Bull while birding at The Scrubs. When the owner finally pulled the beast off me, she had the cheek to say that I was responsible for bringing on the attack by wearing a hat!

Kingfisher

Finding birds

Birds are everywhere, but in order to see them you will need to know where to look and how to search for them. This is certainly the situation in urban areas and is perhaps why so many people shun the idea of there being any birds to be found in our towns and cities. I have frequently taken members of the public on walks around their neighbourhood and been struck by their stunned reactions to the multitude of species that I'm able to show them. Newbie birders are often overawed when they are out with birders more experienced than themselves, some even doubting their ability to have found any birds had they been on their own. Never worry about things like that, as there will soon come the day when you realize that you know more than you thought you did and have seen far more than you've given yourself credit for. Learn at your own pace. No one knows everything, and at one point everybody knew nothing.

There is, however, an art to finding birds, particularly in urban areas. Back in the days when I worked on TV commercials, I was with a film crew on the top floor of a warehouse in east London one summer afternoon. We were shooting an advert and during a period of downtime I was chatting to some of the crew and explained that there were always lots of birds around in the city. They clearly thought I was mad, especially when I cockily claimed that I could find and identify ten different species in ten minutes in that industrial wasteland just by looking through a thin strip of a window that overlooked factory rooftops and some sky. Convinced that I had lost the plot, my colleagues wagered a bet and placed some serious money on the table. The heat was on. Within ten minutes I had shown them a Pied Wagtail, a couple of Swifts, some Starlings, a Magpie, a pair of Carrion Crows, a Greenfinch, a group of Herring and Lesser Black-backed Gulls, a Blackbird and a small flock of Goldfinches. We were all richer for the experience!

Pied Wagtail

Now, let me quickly say that I was not trying to make myself look clever by flaunting my knowledge in order to impress people. There was method in my cockiness: I knew that I could find at least ten species because I was familiar with the types of birds that might inhabit such a barren-looking landscape, and understood where and how to look for them. The best way of learning your birds is by regularly visiting a local patch and ideally a range of different types of habitat. If you put in enough time you will gradually be able to build up a list of the usual suspects. By being aware of your surroundings you will subconsciously realize that the bit of woodland next to your office may be a good place to see Goldcrests, while the river near the shops might be worth scanning for a passing Kingfisher. Soon you will visit similar habitats at other sites and know instinctively which birds to expect. Your knowledge fountain is beginning to flow.

Those birders who seem to see everything and get all the luck have actually had to earn it. They would have invariably spent hours in the field watching over their patches and studying every bird that they happened across. Therein lies the secret of how to become a better birder: getting enough experience in the field. However, this does not mean that you have to be out birding several days a week, as your skills can still be honed as you go about your daily life. The golden rule is always to look closely at every bird you come across, wherever that might be, and to listen to calls and songs to work out what they mean – is it a contact call, song or alarm note? By doing this you will be practicing hand-to-eye coordination with your binoculars, learning more about identification and behaviour, picking up on sounds, and generally noticing birds that you may not have done previously.

Don't be put off looking at birds for fear of not being able to recognize them. There is not one birder on the planet who can confidently put a name to everything that perches up in front of them. If they say they can, then they are fibbers. I have hung out with some of the best observers in the world and they are all fallible. There is nothing wrong with drawing a blank, as some birds just defy identification. Simply enjoy the experience and try to make as many notes as possible. One day you may revisit your notes and suddenly realize that the 'mystery' warbler you saw furtively inspecting the foliage in your apple tree was indeed a Willow Warbler.

An interesting aspect of this learning curve that is not often talked about is the use of peripheral vision. When you look at a bird, also look around it at the same time, and train yourself to be alert to movement at the edges of your visual range. In this way you may notice the Sparrowhawk buzzing the extreme end of the Starling flock you were focused on, or spot the Snipe feeding unobtrusively in the wet meadow near the Moorhen that you were admiring. When you watch a bird such as a Buzzard passing overhead use your peripheral vision to locate any other birds soaring with it. Soon you will be noticing movement from the corner of your eye far more regularly.

I am forever detecting birds in my peripheral vision, often much to the bemusement of the non-birdy people I am with. One summer's day, I was on London's Southbank in the heart of the city and having a discussion with my girlfriend about where to go for lunch. The London Marathon was on and the Thames was awash with boats. Standing side-on to the river while chatting to her I noticed out of the corner of my eye a dark bird diving in the water amongst the boats. I was about to dismiss it as a Cormorant when I noticed, again

Kestrel (female)

Shag

Little Egret

without really focussing on it, that the bird had leapt clean out of the water before diving in. This is classic Shag behaviour, the Cormorant's more maritime relative and an unusual inland visitor. I broke off mid-sentence to confirm that it was in fact an adult Shag – the first and only one that I've ever seen in the London area.

When you watch birds over a prolonged period of time you gradually build up a mental dossier of their behavioural traits. No longer will it 'only' be a Jay that's just landed on a branch in the garden, but a colourful member of the crow family that you personally know quite a lot about. You will have discovered that although ostensibly a shy bird, Jays really know how to work an area when foraging for food and can sometimes allow a fairly close approach. Watching a bird's behaviour, which is what birding is all about by the way, will also help to improve your identification skills no end. For example, you will notice that Dunnocks creep around the foot of the bird table and along the edges of dense cover like mice – no other common bird of its size behaves in the same way. And during the breeding season you see male sparrows puffing up their chests, cocking their tails and chirruping their little heads off as they flick their wings trying to attract the attentions of a female – behaviour that is pretty much unique to House Sparrows.

Recognizing a bird by incorporating the way it acts and behaves into the whole identification mix is how the experts go about their business. It's comparable to the way in which we can instantly recognize a friend or relative walking down the street amongst a crowd of people. Whether we know it or not, we are distinguishing them using a suite of different features: gait, build, facial appearance and, if they come close enough, by their voice. However, it's worth bearing in mind that birds sometimes act out of character, which can make them quite confusing to identify. This is why repeatedly watching birds going about their daily lives really helps to get to know the individual traits of the various species to be found in your area

The ability to find birds is the combination of several aspects of fieldcraft: seeing the habitat around you as a bird would, being observant, listening out, and by using what I regard as 'The Force'. There is undoubtedly a large element of luck involved in birding:

Snipe

Grey Phalarope

sometimes you look over your shoulder and see a bird you wouldn't normally expect; you may subconsciously change your route on the patch and discover a gem; or you may merely be thinking about a bird and seconds later be looking at one. I firmly believe that the more positive your thoughts, the more likely you are to see something interesting – this is what I call using The Force! If you believe that anything can turn up anywhere at anytime, then it will. And if you want to see a particular species on your patch, then one day you will.

Another factor in finding birds is being able see them when others point them out, and conversely to be able to point them out yourself. It may sound obvious but I have so many times heard people say "it's in the tree with the green leaves," which would have been fine had there been only one tree with green leaves, but when that tree is in a wood surrounded by identical trees that's when things start to get a little difficult. I have been guilty of poor directions on many occasions. We all do it. If the vista the bird is sitting in has a couple of describable landmarks then use them: "the Kestrel's sitting in the tree to the right of the blue tower block." If you're on a rooftop and see what you think is a distant Red Kite drifting in from the south, explain roughly where and how far away it is by using landmarks – and also by indicating the direction in which the bird is travelling. A lot of birders use the clock system, whereby directly ahead of you is midday, due right is 3 o'clock and due left is 9 o'clock. Your directions could, therefore, more helpfully be "the Kestrel is sitting in the tree with green leaves that's roughly 2 o'clock from where I'm facing."

Note taking

I saw my first Greylag Geese grazing in a field near Tring Reservoir in Hertfordshire at 08:50hrs on 17th September 1977. They, and my first ever Green Sandpipers, were among the 49 species that I clocked up on that cold, cloudy morning. I can still recall that day vividly, as I can practically every other day that I've been out birding since then. The reason I'm able to do this is because I've been writing field notes ever since I could hold a pen. Well, not quite, but I do have a stack of notebooks spanning nearly 30 years – from my first ever outing up to the day I took to recording sightings electronically. Those notes have become a treasured chronicle that I'm able to refer to whenever I wish, not only to relive my birding experiences but also to remind me of what I was doing at the various stages in my life.

The art of taking notes using pen and paper is sadly a dying one, although it's certainly an art that deserves to be revived. Renowned twitcher, Lee Evans, once lamented that in a whole year spent traversing Britain and Ireland in search of birds he had only seen four birders making notes in the field. I must say that I have noticed this trend too, and then it is usually only someone of the older generation. When I was a kid, going birding without producing a notebook would have been like playing football without a ball.

Keeping notes has a very practical use, since documenting visits to your local patch over a course of a couple of years will begin to show patterns emerging. You will be able to work out when migrant birds are likely to arrive and depart, as well as see how the populations of the species present ebb and flow. That knowledge will give you an added insight to your area that will quickly elevate you to being a local birding expert. Making notes is so easy and the amount of information you record is totally up to you. Ever since I was a kid, my notes have generally consisted of recording the place, date and time of my visit, together with a list of the species and number of individuals seen. I also note down the weather and, where appropriate make comments on behaviour. It really is as simple as that.

There are, of course, varying approaches to making bird notes, and levels to which you can go. Some birders I know never keep a record of anything, preferring instead to commit their sightings to memory. Others have quite complex programs on their computers that involve transferring their field notes onto spreadsheets, and yet others simply write down the more notable birds they see and leave it at that. In recent years there has been an increasing trend for birders to submit their bird tallies using apps such as eBird or Birdtrack. The advantage in doing this is that your records get fed into a real-time database that can give an instant picture as to the state of populations on a regional, national or even global level. These apps also have the facility for your notes to be kept digitally, allowing you to refer back to them whenever you want. With some apps you can even have access to quite complex analyses of your submitted records.

Nowadays, I always have a notebook with me in the field just in case I notice anything unusual, but I otherwise file my species list for the day onto my laptop when I get home. If I do come across a bird that is unfamiliar, I try to note down as many salient points about it as possible. It is important to use words that will make sense to you, particularly if you try to capture the essence of the bird's 'jizz' – its 'feel'. For example, "bounced its tail like a wagtail," "walked in a sedate manner" or "sprinted like it was a clockwork toy." Don't be alarmed if you describe an aspect of behaviour or the overall demeanour of a bird that is not mentioned in the books. What you've witnessed may have been something that is rarely seen or, indeed, may never have been reported before. That would be fantastic – after all you're being an amateur ornithologist, studying birds.

Goshawk

I remember birding at Wormwood Scrubs one day when a Goshawk flew over, hotly pursued by a small gang of crows. I instantly knew that it was a Goshawk as I'd seen them several times before, but this was the first one I'd ever seen in a British urban setting. The standard descriptions in field guides talk about this supreme woodland predator being a large, Buzzard-sized Sparrowhawk (to which it is a close relative) that shares the latter's flap-flap-glide flight action, albeit rather more languid. I echoed those characteristics in my notes, but also mentioned that I felt it had more the general feel of a female Hen Harrier – a bird of open country that characteristically holds its wings in a shallow 'V' when gliding between rather leisurely wingbeats. Since the bird I'd been watching clearly wasn't a Hen Harrier, this may have been an odd note to make, but it did emphasize that it had a very different jizz to that of a Sparrowhawk – the most likely confusion species.

Another note that's useful to make is an indication of the size of the bird you are describing. Try to compare it with another species nearby or, if you feel confident, another species with which you are familiar, even if that species isn't present.

Earlier in this book I included a simplistic diagram of a bird and suggested a very basic way of describing its general features. Once you are familiar with this approach and the general topography of a bird, your note taking can become a little more detailed if you learn to look for certain, more specific, features. So let me introduce a more detailed illustration of a bird with the various parts labelled. Being in contact with other, perhaps more experienced birders is likely to expose you to some of this often strange topographical terminology and if you can it's worth incorporating some into your vernacular. But don't beat yourself up if the terms are not sticking, it is a gradual process and don't worry if you never learn any of them.

When faced with a 'mystery' bird try to describe it as thoroughly as possible, as your notes may help to confirm its identity long after it's gone. In particular, look at the head markings, the overall patterns of streaking or blocks of colour, the length of the wings and tail and any other obvious features. Also make a careful note of the bird's bare parts – its legs and bill. What colour are they? Are they long or short? If the bird calls, try to describe phonetically what you hear, and, finally, jot down any obvious aspects of behaviour – but bear in mind that displaced birds sometimes behave out of character. It's always worth attempting a quick sketch of your 'mystery' bird, indicating the obvious elements of its plumage and general structure. But don't stress if drawing is not your forte – believe me, very few among us can knock out a sketch remotely close to the quality of the work seen in most modern field guides. So long as the main features that you want to highlight are

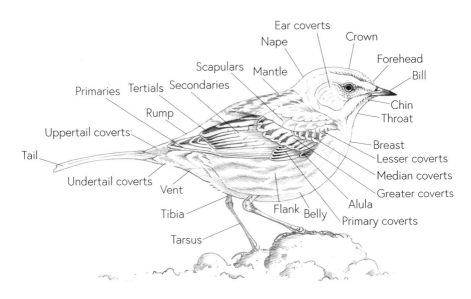

Dunnock

213

emphasized, then it's job done. In my case, I often end up with a distorted and very bad drawing that either resembles a poor attempt at abstract art or a stick insect!

Field notes and sketches will be particularly useful if you are lucky enough to come across a rarity, as in order to be verified, records of such birds are assessed by rarities committees. Unless there is sufficient information to confirm an identification beyond any reasonable doubt, a record is not likely to be accepted onto official lists.

I think it's always a good idea to list everything you see, since what may seem unimportant to you at the time could be of particular interest to others, such as your birding friends, members of local bird clubs, the county bird recorder (the designated person, usually connected to a local bird club, responsible for gathering everybody's sightings and coordinating the production of an annual bird report that is made available to the general public), or national organizations such as the BTO. Indeed, lists of birds form the very basis of several of the BTO's surveys, especially Garden BirdWatch and BirdTrack that collate random lists from birders up and down the country and convert their data into meaningful information on the current distribution of Britain's birds. I'll say a little more about surveys towards the end of this section.

Taking notes in the field is the perfect way to record the immediacy of your sightings. However, using good old-fashioned notebooks has its problems. Rain, in particular, generally puts paid to any note taking. Although rainproof notebooks are available, I've actually never seen anyone using one. If it's bitterly cold you can also forget about writing notes, since even wearing gloves can sometimes prove too cumbersome for any meaningful pen work – always accepting, of course, that your pen will actually work or that the end of your pencil hasn't snapped off!

Note taking has perhaps reached a new level thanks to modern technology. Some people take notes by whispering into a Dictaphone, and the new generation of smartphones have excellent built-in recording facilities. The benefit of voice recording is that you can continuously watch your subject while speaking into the microphone. The disadvantage with this method is that you might have to then transcribe it once you get home – although some voice-recognition software can be very helpful in this respect. However, technology comes into its own when you're standing close to a strange bird that's singing its heart out. You can make a digital recording and then either email, Dropbox or SoundCloud the sound clip to be shared instantaneously with anyone, anywhere in the world. Even though the sound quality won't not come close to what could be achieved using professional equipment,

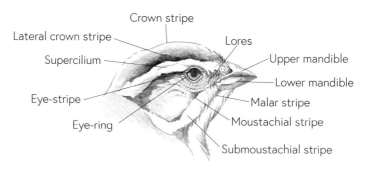

Crown stripe

Lateral crown stripe

Lores

Supercilium

Upper mandible

Lower mandible

Eye-stripe

Malar stripe

Eye-ring

Moustachial stripe

Submoustachial stripe

it can be perfectly adequate for identification. I still have some great recordings on my phone of singing Nightingales and Reed Warblers – and the sound of 10,000 Common Cranes calling at their roosting site in the Hula Valley in Israel, which I still find spine-tingling.

As we know, photography is a major part of modern birding, with more and more people carrying cameras – birds now frequently being identified from photographs, sometimes after the event. However, try not to rely on using your camera as a replacement for your field notes. By that I mean look at an unfamiliar bird as much as possible using your naked eye and optics, and ideally take some mental notes before jotting them down or recording the information in some other way. In an ideal world, only once you've satisfied yourself with the views of the bird should your camera be brought into play – essentially just to reinforce your field observations. Of course, in the real world you never know how long the bird in question will hang around, so you may have to improvise and produce the camera first to secure some record shots, and do the note taking afterwards. Pictures capture a moment in time but not the intricacies of how a bird behaves, so once you've taken a few pictures why not switch your camera to video mode and shoot some footage.

I may be a little old-fashioned, and although technology and photographs clearly have their place, to my mind nothing beats the visceral quality of hand-written notes and sketches. Looking back at my old notebooks always leaves me with the positive feeling that I really did see those birds.

Common Cranes

Migrant birds, such as this Nightjar, can pitch down anywhere ahead of weather fronts.

When to go birding

I've learnt about the best times to go birding through much trial and error, although I soon realized that the first few hours after dawn can be particularly good, especially during spring and autumn. Birds are always up early, taking advantage of the feeding opportunities in the tranquil gardens prior to the first of the back doors being swung open and the hound slung out in order to relieve itself. As I explained in the *Urban garden birding* section, there are peaks and troughs in bird activity, with mornings and late afternoon to early evenings being the most productive times. However, the quietest (in terms of human activity) and therefore optimum time to go urban birding is in the morning, before everybody wakes up. Of course, the time of year will also have a big influence on what you see during your birding sessions.

If you live in a coastal town or city, it's definitely worth getting to know how to use a tide table; these are readily available online or from local outlets for all parts of the UK. At low tide waders and gulls might be feeding way out on the exposed mud, far from the shore. But if you time your visit carefully, you may be able to watch these birds being forced towards you as the tide rises. Spring tides have the largest ranges, particularly if they coincide with a full or new moon.

However, the rules governing the best time to go birding can be thrown out of the window if the weather is dreadful and it's blowing a hooley, as there's little point in venturing out at all in such conditions. Once a weather front has passed, though, it's always worth heading out straight away, particularly during the migration season, as you never know what might have been brought in. Birds usually travel ahead of weather fronts and often pitch

A sketch map of a typical local patch

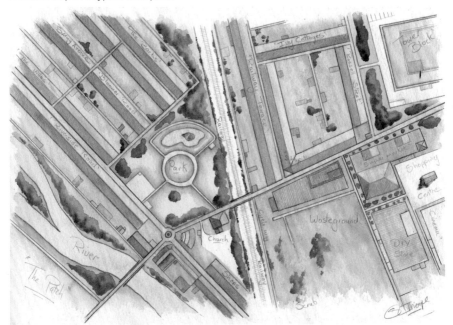

down into the nearest shelter to ride out the worst of the conditions, so who knows what treats may be in store at your local patch. On several occasions I've seen oddities such as Little Ringed Plovers, Curlew and Whimbrel feeding incongruously on waterlogged football pitches after a storm. I have also discovered Cuckoos that have been stalled by bad weather, including one that kept flying steadily north one spring, even through very heavy rain.

I will never forget reading an account of an urban birder visiting Barn Elms Reservoir, the site that is now the London Wetland Centre, after a terrific spring thunderstorm. He arrived to see a good number of Black Terns (a scarce migrant at the best of times) feeding low over the water, having been brought down by the storm. However, with these terns was a Gull-billed Tern, a major rarity in the UK, that had dropped in briefly before heading off to continue its journey. Migration time is always unpredictable and it therefore pays to keep your eyes peeled at all time.

Finding a local patch

In my opinion, you can't become a birder, urban or otherwise, without having a local patch – and finding one is so easy. Simply take a walk around your local neighbourhood and search for a suitable area close to your home or place of work – and start visiting it whenever you can. Your patch could be a park, stretch of river, local reservoir, a cemetery or almost any open space. Try to pay a visit a few times a week and follow the same route each time. Don't expect to see everything the first time you go there but be patient, since your new patch is unlikely to reveal all its secrets straight away. Eventually, you will get to know the lie of the land and work out where most of the local resident birds are to be found. You may discover a quiet, bushy corner that's a haven for Song Thrushes, Robins and migrant warblers. Or if your patch has a body of water with a reedy section, winter visits may produce Reed Buntings or maybe even a secretive Water Rail.

Having a local patch is a great way to get to grips with watching birds at your own pace in a familiar place. You will find that every new species of bird you discover will be cause for celebration. I suppose my very first patch was my backyard. I literally spent years studying my garden bird populations from my bedroom window before and after primary school. During this time my garden, and those of the neighbours attracted birds that I'd never seen before. I spied my first Goldcrest near the top of a conifer that was very close to my bedroom window and felt elated. I also discovered Reed Buntings, a Lesser Spotted Woodpecker and, best of all, on one April morning my first Common Redstart. It was a gorgeous male that had taken a break while migration north to hop up my garden path, quivering its tail with every bound!

My first real patch was Monks Park, a small urban park two blocks away from my home. A concrete-bedded river ran through it, providing me with my first Moorhens, and on the adjacent derelict land (sadly now long built upon) wintering flocks of Tree Sparrows gathered. Visiting this park practically every day was a great apprenticeship for me, and proved that an overwhelming variety of birds could be seen on my doorstep. I have been a loyal fan of patch-watching ever since. Over the course of a year, with regular visits you will notice changes in the populations of birds, with migrant visitors such as Swallows, Wheatears and Willow Warblers making spring and autumn appearances. During the winter months your patch may play host to roving flocks of Fieldfares and Redwings. And

Willow Warbler

Wormwood Scrubs, London

if there are playing fields nearby these may attract flocks of loafing gulls. You may even get lucky and flush a Snipe from a boggy area. It will be a great training ground and you will soon be able to recognize the common birds on your patch with relative ease and, better still, without realizing it. Nothing beats the feeling of finding a new bird for your patch, no matter how common it is. It will be 'your' bird – found by you and no one else.

Don't worry if your chosen patch doesn't resemble a birding paradise teeming with thousands of beauties. Although you may see next to nothing during some visits, don't be put off and persevere. Even on the quiet days I guarantee that you will see something that you've never seen before. This may not necessarily be a new species, but more likely a bird you thought you already knew doing something different.

I have had several local patches during my life and Wormwood Scrubs, my current one, at first glance looks like one of the most unlikely places to find birds. It is essentially a bunch of football pitches surrounded by the thinnest strip of relatively young woodland. During the 25 years that I have birded The Scrubs I've found over 150 species, which is not bad for a site with no standing water and encircled by urbanity. I have been amazed at some of the birds I've found there: waders like Whimbrel, Common Sandpiper and even Greenshank; London scarcities such as breeding Lesser Whitethroats; and even a Richard's Pipit, the national scarcity I mentioned earlier that normally resides in Asia. I even recorded Britain's second-ever overwintering Common Redstart a few days before Christmas in 2006. I still dine out on that one! Yet again, this just goes to show that anything can turn up anywhere at anytime – especially if you open your mind to the possibilities.

Over the months and years your sightings may attract the attentions of other birders, and although you might have a slight inclination to want to keep your patch to yourself, do welcome them as more eyes equates to more birds. Eventually, if there are enough records you might be able to prove that your patch is a locally important site and increase the chances of it being protected from encroaching development.

Despite the fact that you may go on to become well travelled in your pursuit of birds, regardless of where you are in the world you will look forward to walking your patch in the mornings when you return home. You will also vehemently resist any attempts by anyone to threaten the peace in your haven. Once you start to have these feelings you will know that you've truly found your local patch.

Carrion Crows

Listing and reporting your sightings

Although birders come in all shapes, sizes and hues, the one thing they tend to have in common is a propensity for making lists. In fact, I know very few birders who don't keep lists and even these people probably keep a mental note of the birds they've seen. Anyone who actively keeps lists of the birds or other things they've recorded becomes what's known as a Lister – and this can develop into an obsession!

When I was younger I used to keep all sorts of bird lists. I had lists for my garden, local patch, office, whilst playing football, London, Britain and Ireland, and the world. As a kid, imaginary lists were also part of the deal so I would write lists of the birds that I thought occurred in random countries like Finland and Albania. As I grew older and ventured farther afield I also kept lists of all the birds that I saw in various parts of the world – whether on 'temporary' local patches if I was staying in a town or city, or trekking through the jungles of Peru. And even to this day I still make lists. Although these lists were initially recorded in cheap notebooks bought from the local newsagent, now, as I explained earlier, I store them on my computer.

Lists are a very personal thing and it is totally up to you how you go about it. The types of lists that most birders keep include garden, local patch, county, national and world (life) lists, although year lists are also very popular. In my youth I had plenty of time to make all sorts of lists, as there were far fewer distractions from things like the Internet and playing with smartphones. However, I'm a still a firm advocate of listing for the very reasons I've already explained.

Hoopoe

Some people only put a bird on their list – or tick it, to use proper birding parlance – if they have seen it, whilst others also include the birds that they've heard. If you want to take your listing to the next level, there are a few websites, such as BUBO Listing and HBW Alive (Handbook of the Birds of the World), that have ready-made lists following the taxonomic views of the major authorities in this field. Some birders take their lists very seriously and see them as the ultimate currencies to prove how good a birder they are. In reality, though, you can be a good birder no matter how many or how few species you've seen. All that matters is that you enjoy what you do.

Urban birder or urban twitcher?

The term twitcher can be a very contentious one, often used by the media as a trivializing blanket term to cover everyone with any sort of interest in birds. Twitchers get twitchy is an often used and very boring headline! There is a difference between a birder and a twitcher and neither is better nor worse than the other. It is interesting to note that birders can twitch and twitchers bird. Generally speaking, birders have a local patch and go birding there and farther afield when the opportunity arises, whereas twitchers are keen listers and, as such, are particularly interested in adding to their lists. Once you've seen all the common birds, there will obviously only be the rarer ones left to see. So twitchers have to traverse the country in order to see a new species for their list – known as a tick or a lifer. Legend has it that the term twitching originated in the 50s when birders arriving at the site of a reported rarity would get off their motorbikes and twitch excitedly. Today, the mere mention of the word twitching can result in surprising reactions. Some birders are vehemently opposed to even being considered a twitcher, whereas those in the twitching fraternity are fiercely proud of their pursuit.

Broadly speaking, a twitcher teeters between being very interested and a total obsessive when it comes to adding species to their life lists habitually chasing after hopelessly lost rarities. It is a predominantly male pursuit and an expensive one at that, with some exponents thinking nothing of chartering aircraft at short notice to ferry them to and from far-flung

Rarities, such as the White-rumped Sandpiper from America, always get hearts racing when they make landfall in the UK.

destinations within the UK in the hope of picking up that mystical lifer. This obsession can sometimes take over one's psyche and has, famously, ruined marriages, friendships, work prospects, cars and bank accounts. I think it's fair to say that most birders have twitched at some time in their birding lives. If an unusual, although not necessarily particularly rare bird, turns up at your local patch and you go to look for it then, technically, you are twitching. I went through a brief twitching phase during the 80s and openly admit that my pager, which alerted me to new rarities, ruled my life. I remember once being in Suffolk watching a Red-rumped Swallow that hails from southern Europe – but only briefly as suddenly my pager buzzed and I found myself bundling into a speeding car with other twitchers Dorset-bound to tick off a newly discovered Terek Sandpiper, a rare wader from the east, as the light faded.

Twitching invariably involves standing around, sometimes for hours, in all types of weather. There is also the anxiety of whether the bird will show or, indeed, ever be seen again. If you're contemplating twitching, don't expect to see every bird you chase after, as it may be disturbed, decide to move on of its own volition or even expire, scuppering your chances even before you arrive. To maximize your chances of seeing a rarity, it's therefore always best to arrive on the day the bird is reported, as most migrants tend to move on overnight, especially if it is clear and moonlit.

Then there are the crowds, ranging from a handful of people if the bird is not particularly rare, or if you happen to be in Ireland where there are relatively few birders, to mass twitches attended by literally hundreds, and sometimes even thousands of birders. Perhaps the most famous twitch of all time was in 1989 when a North American Golden-winged Warbler turned up in a Tesco car park in Aylesford, Kent – the only one ever recorded in the UK.

If you want to become a twitcher then there are several easy steps to take. The first is to take out a subscription with one of the rare bird information apps like Rare Bird Alert or BirdGuides. Then configure the app so that you receive the type of news you want to hear about, be it national or regional rarities – once the news starts coming through your heart will be in your mouth. Perspiration and stress will kick in when you discover that Britain's first Eskimo Curlew in 130 years has just been found on Fair Isle and you are about to go into a meeting.

Be warned, as twitching can be very addictive. Try to garner a relationship with an understanding partner who will not get too uptight if you dumped them at the altar or rush off when they're sick to tick some lost Siberian waif. Unfortunately, such spouses probably don't exist – so if you want to be a hardcore twitcher then maybe you'd be better off remaining single! However, despite being very competitive, twitchers seldom act alone, so find some like-minded buddies in order to at least share petrol, ferry and aviation fuel costs.

To be a twitcher it is not essential to have a good knowledge of birds initially, as much can be learned in the field from other, more experienced birders or twitchers. However, it pays to 'gen-up' on the particular species that you are wishing to see so that you will know what to expect when the Philadelphia Vireo that you've been staking out for the past five hours sticks its head out of a bush.

Of course, you don't have to be a hardcore twitcher to enjoy the thrill of seeing a rare bird. Some birders, like myself, are far more interested in being finders. The most rewarding feeling as a birder is to put in countless hours at your local patch until that momentous day when you discover a national rarity. Other birders work on the premise that if there happens to be a rarity close to where they are, it would be rude not to pay it a visit.

But regardless of what kind of rare bird watching you engage in, always remember to put the welfare of the bird first. Never flush a bird deliberately, and certainly not incessantly, as it's probably dog-tired after a long flight. Similarly, avoid the temptation to approach too closely with a camera. Also, it's important to respect the privacy of landowners and other residents who live in the area, and never to risk damaging crops, boundary fencing or walls in an attempt to get a better view of a bird.

Hooking up with other birders

Nowadays, birding, and in particular urban birding, can be quite a social occasion. Indeed, urban birding was recently described as the 'new rock 'n' roll' on the front pages of two high class magazines, *Condé Nast Traveller* and *Shortlist Magazine*. You may wonder why. Well, as this book has hopefully revealed, birding is fun and rewarding, it's easy to get involved – and as you'll soon discover there *are* plenty of birds to be found in urban areas. Urban birding certainly has a cool allure about it. Sure, it's possible to spend quiet, contemplative moments on your own birding, especially if you get to your patch very early in the morning. But when starting out there is much to be learned by plugging in to established birding groups.

Black Redstarts are always a great find whilst surveying for breeding birds (this is a juvenile).

Your nearest nature reserve can be a good place to link up with other birders, and you may find that there are organized walks around the site led by the local warden or experienced volunteers. A search online may reveal the existence of local bird clubs and/or RSPB groups, all of which are keen to welcome newcomers and many arrange trips to birding sites near and far – a great way of meeting new birding buddies. You can also make your birding more than just a casual pastime by becoming actively involved in conservation work on local sites.

Cuckoo

Twitches, too, can be fun social occasions, where old friends meet to discuss the latest birding news and reminisce about past twitches, often jibing colleagues who managed to dip (not see) the bird in question!

Surveys and studies

One of the easiest, and most valuable ways of contributing to the birding scene is to get involved in survey work. Even if your local patch doesn't extend beyond your garden, you can still participate in the RSPB's Big Garden Birdwatch, which, as I mentioned earlier, entails spending an hour identifying and counting the birds visiting your garden on one day during the last weekend in January. And you can do this from the comfort of your kitchen over a nice cup of tea. Or, as I've explained previously, you can 'add value' to your birding by entering your species lists online onto BirdTrack, hosted by the BTO, every time you've been out. If you want to get even more involved, though, particularly if you're prepared to commit a little more time on a regular basis, you could always contribute to BTO surveys that rely on repeat visits, such as the Breeding Bird Survey.

As trivial as you may think your records may be, they are in fact vital in the bigger scheme of things. It's equally important to record negative as well as positive results from your survey – such as not seeing a House Sparrow or finding a complete absence of Black-headed Gulls when previously you were practically tripping over them. Information like this may, for example, reflect population peaks and troughs or provide a valuable insight into the arrival and departure dates of migrants.

Some people have a particular interest in a certain species or group of species, and spend pretty much all their time studying the various aspects of the birds' behaviour. Such an interest may start by studying the antics of the Robins in the garden, making mental notes, perhaps taking pictures and reading all the reference material available. One day you may notice your Robin doing something that was not covered anywhere in the literature, and thereafter become totally obsessed. You don't need to have a doctorate to be able to contribute to the scientific knowledge base, as amateur ornithologists have made many important discoveries over the years. At the very least, by focussing on your chosen species you will gain a rewarding and intimate connection with it that few other people will have shared.

The study of migration has become a sexy subject again in fairly recent years, mainly due to technological advances in the use of geotags. These are small biodegradable radio transmitters with a short protruding aerial that the bird wears like a rucksack. The transmitters emit a signal that can be picked up by orbiting satellites and enable the bird's position to be tracked anywhere on earth. The data obtained from tracking birds in this way has been astonishing. For example, it has been found that Cuckoos spend just a few weeks in the UK before making the return journey to Africa, and that individual birds follow different migration routes from one year to the next. With information like this becoming available, our understanding of the movements of birds is increasing all the time, providing essential evidence that can be used to help protect them on their breeding and wintering grounds, as well as at key staging posts during their migration.

Although data on the migration of birds can be collated from observational records, such as 'vis migging' (visible migration watching to you and I), more detailed information can be obtained by ringing individual birds. This involves placing uniquely numbered rings on their legs and is undertaken mainly by specially trained volunteers. Birds are generally caught in mist nets and information recorded on the species and location of capture for each of the rings fitted. Whenever possible, details of the sex and age of the bird, and other so-called biometric data (measurements of various parts of the bird's anatomy), are also recorded. The information garnered from recovered birds can be very exciting indeed, such as the discovery of a ringed Manx Shearwater caught on a rocky Welsh coastline that was at least 55 years old! It is stories like this, and the results of geotagging studies, that seem to particularly enthrall the media.

Long-eared Owls

In the UK, the ringing scheme is administered by the BTO and you should contact them if you want to find out about getting involved with a ringing group near you. Volunteering to become a ringer is very worthwhile and enjoyable, but since it takes several years to learn the ropes with a licensed trainer, you do need to be prepared to make a serious time commitment.

Volunteering

Finally, you could always dedicate some of your spare time to volunteering on a nature reserve. There are many angles you could pursue, depending on your skills and interests. Rolling your sleeves up to help shape and manage the habitats is a direct way of getting involved, as is trying to galvanize people into supporting your conservation efforts, whether financially or physically. Whatever you feel able to contribute will be beneficial in helping to conserve our precious wildlife.

Urban birding abroad

OK, so you've learnt the basics about British birds and birding, know what attire to don, how to use your binoculars and, importantly, become familiar with the kinds of urban habitats that are most likely to be good for birds. You might, though, now have the urge to take the next step and travel overseas to watch birds. There are many great urban birding destinations throughout the world – and if you apply the same principles as I've outlined in this book, take extra care and hook up with local birders, you're sure to have a wonderful holiday and see many more fantastic birds!

Blue Rock Thrush

Just give it a go!

It is pretty amazing that within the space of a decade birding in the UK has shed its perhaps rather fuddy-duddy image and become, dare I say, a very sexy pastime. As I have said throughout this book, watching birds in our towns and cities is a great way to de-stress from the pressures of urban life, even if it is only for ten minutes in a day. Indeed, urban birding has a tremendously meditative and calming effect – a response I have seen many times over the years from a wide range of people.

I recall taking a non-birder on a walk around The Scrubs, my patch, one summer's afternoon. As we left I noticed a bunch of six bantering youths either sitting on or leaning against my car that was parked on the street bordering the site. Naturally, my companion was nervous when he saw what was going on and advised that we come back later. I wasn't as apprehensive, though, and told him to follow me as I approached them. The kids stopped talking and glared at me menacingly as I offered them a friendly greeting. "What are you doing? Bird watching?" sneered one of them, much to the amusement of the rest of his mates. "Yes I am actually," I responded, "and I bet that none of you can use my binoculars to track and follow those Swifts that are flying above our heads right now."

The lads immediately stared up into the sky to witness a party of Swifts, no doubt local breeders, swirling erratically on the air currents. One guy reached out for my binoculars and then began an unlikely episode as each took his turn in trying to follow the birds using my optics. They were laughing and celebrating when they momentarily got a bird in sight while I gave them a breakdown of how remarkable Swifts were, as well as instructions on how to

Starling

Swifts

use the binoculars as proficiently as possible. Soon, they were commenting on how much fun it was and I noted that a least one of them was really engaged. In the end the guys were chatting away about their newly found discovery in life, the Swift. Later, my companion admitted that he was really worried initially, thinking that we were going to have an incident on our hands. But I had no such concerns because I believed in the power of birds!

Birds can warm any cold heart, raise low spirits, turn frowns to smiles and bring love into your life. Birds are an incredible conduit, with the ability to touch even the most confirmed of urbanites by providing that connection with the world that envelopes us: nature.

In 2015 I conducted a nationwide poll to elect Britain's National Bird. This resulted in over 250,000 members of the great British public voting. Most of the voters weren't denizens of the countryside, but people living mainly in urban centres. Remarkably, fewer than 40% were members of any of the NGOs (non-governmental organizations) like the National Trust or even the RSPB. The majority were ordinary people who had probably never pointed a pair of binoculars in the direction of a bird in their lives. Yet they were talking about birds, and noticing birds in their gardens and around their neighbourhood.

To be an urban birder you don't have to have an encyclopedic knowledge and spend hours every day in the field. You don't have to change your lifestyle, shun friends or wear green. All you have to do is become an urban explorer. Treat your local area as a tract of wilderness and see it through the eyes of a bird. Discover hitherto unknown habitats and study the birds that use those areas. With the help of this book I hope you will uncover a whole new world.

So just get out there and give it a go – and don't forget to look up!

ACKNOWLEDGEMENTS AND PHOTO CREDITS

The research for this book would not have been possible without the valued help from my many friends from across the globe. There are far too many to mention but those listed below are people who really made a huge difference for me. I am indebted to you all! Niklas Aronsson, Jim & Joel Ashton aka The Butterfly Brothers, Rob Ayers, Fiona Barclay, Jo Carlton, David (DC) Chandler, Brian Clews, Joe Coggins (Canal & River Trust), Clare Evans, David Fettes, Paul Hackett, Wendy Hurrell, David La Puma, Olive May Lindo, Vanesa Palacios, Adam Rogers, Lee Saxby, Viv Schuster, Rick Simpson, Jane Turnbull and Matthew A. Young.

Special thanks to my friends at the London Camera Exchange – Adrian Deary, Nick Richens and Alan Saunders; Leica – Viktoria Franklin, Jason Heward, Nora Marschall, Nanette Roland, Robin Sinha and Mark Symes; RSPB – Richard Bashford, John Day, Adrian Thomas and Juliette Young; and the BTO – Kate Risely and Nick Moran.

Steph' Thorpe deserves extra special thanks for the amazing illustrations to be found throughout the book. She is an extraordinary talent and I feel so fortunate to have met her. This book would not have been the same without her input.

I would also like to thank my friends at Princeton University Press and **WILD**Guides for believing in this book idea. In particular Robert Kirk, Andy Swash and Julia Hall, and especially Rob and Rachel Still for designing it.

A massive heartfelt bundle of gratitude for Andy & Gill Swash who slaved over this book even during their holiday birding in Brazil! You guys made all the difference.

And finally, a huge shout out for a true friend and one of the major influences in my urban birding career, Jamie Oliver. You are truly one in a million. x

This book is greatly enhanced by the wonderful photographs that adorn the pages. Urban bird photography has now become an art form in its own right and I thank all the photographers who have kindly allowed their work to be featured. In total, 271 photographs appear in the book, contributed by 75 photographers, as listed below in alphabetical order by surname:

Peter Alfrey: Urban canal (*p. 36*). **Rubén Cebrián Alonso:** Red Kite (*p. 58*), Telescope backpack (*p. 177*), Snipe (*p. 209*), Tawny Owl (*p. 6*), Kingfisher (*p. 24*), Wren (*p. 27*), Oystercatchers (*p. 51*), Great Tit (*p. 159*), Binoculars (*p. 166*), Golden Oriole (*p. 191*). **Magnus Andersson:** Black-headed Gull (*p. 82*). **Ben Andrew:** Kingfisher (*p. 4*), Kittiwakes (*p. 35*), Cormorants (*p. 42*), Cormorant (*p. 101*), Cormorant (*p. 106*). **Jim Ashton:** Urban garden (*p. 26*), Buddleja (*p. 155*). **Phil Aylen:** Robin (*p. 25*), Tawny Owl (*p. 45*), Grey Heron (*p. 106*), Sparrowhawk (*p. 107*), Chaffinch (*p. 126*), Black Redstart (*p. 137*), Black Redstart (*p. 162*). **Robert Barker University Photography:** Merlin App (*p. 193*). **Tom Bell:** Blackbird (*p. 87*), Starling (*p. 94*), Great Tit (*p. 133*), Grey Squirrel (*p. 145*). **Brita Berbig:** Jackdaw (Front cover). **Blickwinkel / Alamy Stock Photo:** Installing a nestbox for Grey Wagtails (*p. 150*). **Paul Boak:** Using telescope (*p. 173*). **Tomos Brangwyn:** Barn Owl (*p. 160*). **Emily Broad:** Starling (*p. 228*). **Andrew Brown:** Kingfisher (*p. 204*). **Tom Cadwallender:** House Sparrow (*p. 75*). **Roger and Liz Charlwood** (WorldWildlifeImages.com): Wheatear (*p. 8*). **Mark Chrimes:** Peregrine (*p. 108*). **Chris2766 / Shutterstock:** Long-tailed Tit (*p. 117*). **Commission Air / Alamy Stock Photo:** Heathrow Airport (*p. 65*). **Andy Cook:** Pied Wagtail (*p. 119*). **Greg & Yvonne Dean** (WorldWildlifeImages.com): Turtle Dove (*p. 93*), Blackcap (*p. 120*). **Tony Duckett:** Common Buzzard (*p. 13*), Wheatear (*p. 32*), Willow Warbler (*p. 219*). **Garden Photo World / Alamy Stock Photo:** London rush hour (*p. 19*). **Geogphotos / Alamy Stock Photo:** River Orwell (*p. 33*). **Iestyn George:** Using telescope (*p. 174*), Using telescope (*p. 175*). **June Green / Alamy Stock Photo:** Gunnersbury Triangle Nature Reserve (*p. 49*). **Marc Guyt** (Agami. nl): Swift (*p. 23*), Monk Parakeet (*p. 81*). **Robert Harding / Alamy Stock Photo:** Pembridge Road, Notting Hill (*p. 7*). **Penny Hayhurst:** Using telescope (*p. 177*). **Paul Heyes - Alamy Stock Photo:** Urban wildflower meadow (*p. 49*). **Dave Hollinshead:** House Martin nestbox (*p. 147*). **Rob Hume:** Bookshelf (*p. 163*). **Peter Jones:** Black Redstart (*p. 62*), Sparrowhawk (*p. 151*). **Gideon Knight:** Ring-billed Gull (*p. 31*), Teal (*p. 31*), Green Woodpecker (*p. 45*), Grey Wagtails (*p. 54*), Feral Pigeon (*p. 69*), Feral Pigeons (mixed couple) (*p. 71*), Ring-necked Parakeet on railing (*p. 73*), Herring Gull (*p. 77*), Blackbird (*p. 89*), Canada Geese (*p. 102*), Robin (*p. 131*), Blue Tit (*p. 136*), Ross's Gull (*p. 188*), Kestrel (female) (*p. 207*), Little Egret (*p. 208*), Grey Phalarope (*p. 209*), Carrion Crow (*p. 220*). **Jip Louwe Kooijmans:** Using binoculars (*p. 173*). **Geslin Laurent:** Kingfisher (*p. 39*), Kestrel (*p. 107*). **LCE images:** Binoculars (both) (*p. 167*), Tripod (*p. 175*), Cameras (both) (*p. 180*), Cameras (both) (*p. 181*). **Wil Leurs** (Agami.nl): Peregrine (Fronticepiece). **David Lindo:** Nature Reserve (*p. 8*), Books (*p. 15*), House Sparrow (*p. 18*), Blackbird chicks (*p. 27*), Mute Swan (*p. 31*), Woodberry Reservoir (*p. 37*), Little Ringed Plover (*p. 39*), Kensal Green Cemetery (*p. 44*), Fieldfare (*p. 56*), Common Buzzards (*p. 56*), Tree Sparrow (*p. 59*), Carrion Crow (*p. 65*), Sky (*p. 67*), Feral Pigeon (squab) (*p. 71*), Feral Pigeon (pied form) (*p. 71*), Ring-necked Parakeet roost (*p. 100*), Wood Pigeon (*p. 133*), House Sparrow (*p. 135*), Fieldfare (*p. 137*), Starling (*p. 141*), Song Thrush (*p. 142*), House Martin (*p. 149*), Blackbird (*p. 164*), Common Redstart (*p. 182*), Vignetting (*p. 184*), Lightroom (*p. 185*), Internet (*p. 187*), Using a smartphone (*p. 190*), Dog (*p. 203*), Shag (*p. 208*), Common Cranes (*p. 215*), Urban sunrise (*p. 216*). **Nicole Lindo:** Nightjar (*p. 216*). **Luke Massey:** Feral Pigeon (*p. 11*), London from the air (*p. 20*), Hyde Park and Kensington Gardens (*p. 30*), Coots (*p. 38*), London from the air (*p. 40*), London from the air (*p. 53*), Feral Pigeons (*p. 72*), Grey Heron (*p. 90*), Wormwood Scrubs (*p. 219*), Black Redstart (*p. 224*). **Gretchen Mattison / Alamy Stock Photo:** London Plane (*p. 43*).

Jay McGowan: Oregon Junco (*p. 80*). Jeff Morgan 04 / Alamy Stock Photo: Building site (*p. 61*). Steve Morgan / Alamy Stock Photo: Shopping centre car park (*p. 64*). David Morrision: Peregrine (*p. 52*). Christian Neumann: Goshawk (*p. 125*). Geoff Nutter: 'Vis migging' from Tower 42 (*p. 95*). Arnau Ramos Oviedo / Alamy Stock Photo: Goldfinch (*p. 9*). Vanesa Palacios: Using binoculars (*p. 168*), Wearing shades (*p. 198*), Birding from hide (*p. 201*). Lassi Rautiainen: Hide setup (*p. 179*). Susana Sanroman: David Lindo (Back cover). Ran Schols (Agami.nl): Swift (*p. 114*). Ilse Schrama: Recording bird sound (*p. 186*). Robin Sinha: Using binoculars (*p. 7*), Holding camera (*p. 49*). Russell F. Spencer: Looking up! (*p. 12*), Gazing through window (*p. 14*), Note taking (*p. 16*), Watching a Robin (*p. 20*), Mistle Thrush (*p. 29*), Mallards (*p. 34*), Black-headed Gull (*p. 37*), Canada Geese (*p. 37*), Birding on Tower 42 (*p. 55*), Cormorant (*p. 57*), Little Egret (*p. 60*), Waxwings (*p. 64*), Black-headed Gulls (*p. 67*), Red Kites (*p. 76*), Red Grouse (*p. 78*), Swallow (*p. 92*), Waxwings (*p. 93*), Goldcrest (*p. 94*), Garden (*p. 129*), Long-tailed Tit (*p. 134*), Blackcap (*p. 137*), Bullfinch (*p. 138*), Goldfinch (*p. 140*), Using binoculars (*p. 165*), Urban birding (*p. 171*), Peregrine feeding site (*p. 189*), Breaking the skyline (*p. 202*), Taking notes (*p. 212*), White-rumped Sandpiper (*p. 222*), Gathering of birders (*p. 223*). SPK / Alamy Stock Photo: Sewage farm (*p. 59*). Donna Cordon Stacey: Greenfinch (*p. 153*). Andy & Gill Swash (WorldWildlifeImages.com): Great Crested Grebes (*p. 41*), Canford Heath (*p. 46*), Stonechat (*p. 47*), Little Ringed Plover (*p. 52*), Feral Pigeon (chequered form) (*p. 71*), Feral Pigeon (blue barred form) (*p. 71*), Ring-necked Parakeet on feeder (*p. 73*), Mute Swans (*p. 102*), Mallards (*p. 103*), Tufted Ducks (*p. 104*), Great Crested Grebes (*p. 104*), Moorhen (*p. 105*), Coot (*p. 105*), Herring Gull (*p. 109*), Lesser Black-backed Gull (*p. 109*), Black-headed Gull (*p. 109*), Wood Pigeons (*p. 110*), Feral Pigeon (*p. 110*), Collared Dove (*p. 111*), Ring-necked Parakeet (*p. 112*), Swift (*p. 114*), Swallow (*p. 115*), Great Tit (*p. 116*), Blue Tit (*p. 116*), Robin (*p. 117*), Song Thrush (*p. 118*), Blackbird (*p. 118*), Goldcrest (*p. 120*), Dunnock (*p. 121*), Jay (*p. 122*), Magpie (*p. 122*), Jackdaw (*p. 123*), Carrion Crow (*p. 123*), Starling (*p. 124*), House Sparrow (male) (*p. 125*), Goldfinch (*p. 126*), Blackbird (*p. 132*), House Sparrow (*p. 145*), Domestic Cat (*p. 152*), Blackbird (*p. 156*), Garden pond (*p. 157*), Common Toad (*p. 158*), Holding binoculars (*p. 169*), Nuthatch (*p. 199*), Swifts (*p. 229*). David Tipling (birdphoto. co.uk): Suburban area, Norwich (*p. 25*), Herring Gull (*p. 50*), Robin (*p. 86*), Starling roost at Palace Pier, Brighton (*p. 99*), Tawny Owl (*p. 113*), Pied Wagtail roost (*p. 119*), Wren (*p. 121*), Starling murmuration (*p. 124*), Greenfinch (*p. 127*), Greenfinches and Great Tit (*p. 128*), Platform feeder (*p. 144*), Nest boxes (both) (*p. 146*), Open-fronted nest box (*p. 147*), Nest box in situ (*p. 148*), Inside a nest box (*p. 150*), Cuckoo (*p. 225*). Universal Images Group North America LLC / Alamy Stock Photo: Gulls at a landfill site (*p. 63*). Harvey van Diek (Agami.nl): Great Spotted Woodpecker (*p. 111*). Markus Varesvuo: Wood Pigeons (*p. 96*), House Martin (*p. 115*), Wheatear (*p. 119*). Alex Vargas (Agami.nl): Chicken (*p. 11*). Čeda Vučković: Long-eared Owls (*p. 226*). Nicholas Watts, Vine House Farm: Bird food (three images) (*p. 142*), Bird food (four images) (*p. 143*), Grey Squirrel (*p. 151*). Mandy West: Meadow Pipit (*p. 88*), House Martin (*p. 91*), Robin (*p. 136*). Paul White - South East England / Alamy Stock Photo: Housing development, Milton Keynes (*p. 136*). Marc Zakian / Alamy Stock Photo: Olympic Park Velodrome (*p. 23*).

In addition, the following images are reproduced under the terms of the Creative Commons Attribution 2.0 UK Generic License:

Bob Edwards (flickr.com/photos/pictureliverpool): Princes Park, Toxteth (*p. 28*); Susanne Nilsson (flickr.com/photos/infomastern): House Sparrow (female) (*p. 125*); Tony Smith (flickr. com/photos/pc_plod): Long-tailed Tit (*p. 49*).